Marketing and Outreach for the Academic Library

Creating the 21st-Century Academic Library

About the Series

Creating the 21st-Century Academic Library provides both conceptual information and practical guidance on the full spectrum of innovative changes now underway in academic libraries. Each volume in the series is carefully crafted to be a hallmark of professional practice and thus:

- Focuses on one narrowly defined aspect of academic librarianship.
- Features an introductory chapter, surveying the content to follow and highlighting lessons to be learned.
- Shares the experiences of librarians who have recently overseen significant changes in their library to better position it to provide 21st-century services to students, faculty, and researchers.

About the Series Editor

Bradford Lee Eden is one of librarianship's most experienced and knowledgeable editors. Dr. Eden is dean of library services at Valparaiso University. Previous positions include associate university librarian for technical services and scholarly communication at the University of California, Santa Barbara; head of web and digitization services and head of bibliographic and metadata services for the University of Nevada, Las Vegas Libraries. He is editor of *OCLC Systems & Services: International Digital Library Perspectives* and *The Bottom Line: Managing Library Finances*, and he is on the editorial boards of *Library Hi Tech* and the *Journal of Film Music*. He is currently the editor of *Library Leadership & Management*, the journal of the Library Leadership & Management Association (LLAMA) within ALA.

Titles in the Series

1. *Leading the 21st-Century Academic Library: Successful Strategies for Envisioning and Realizing Preferred Futures*
2. *Enhancing Teaching and Learning in the 21st-Century Academic Library: Successful Innovations That Make a Difference*
3. *Cutting-Edge Research in Developing the Library of the Future*
4. *Creating Research Infrastructures in the 21st-Century Academic Library*
5. *Partnerships and New Roles in the 21st-Century Academic Library: Collaborating, Embedding, and Cross-Training for the Future*
6. *Rethinking Technical Services: New Frameworks, New Skill Sets, New Tools, New Roles*
7. *Marketing and Outreach for the Academic Library: New Approaches and Initiatives*
8. *Envisioning Our Preferred Future: New Services, Jobs, and Directions*

Marketing and Outreach for the Academic Library

New Approaches and Initiatives

Edited by
Bradford Lee Eden

ROWMAN & LITTLEFIELD
Lanham • Boulder • New York • London

Published by Rowman & Littlefield
A wholly owned subsidiary of The Rowman & Littlefield Publishing Group, Inc.
4501 Forbes Boulevard, Suite 200, Lanham, Maryland 20706
www.rowman.com

Unit A, Whitacre Mews, 26-34 Stannary Street, London SE11 4AB

British Library Cataloguing in Publication Information Available

Library of Congress Cataloging-in-Publication Data

Names: Eden, Bradford Lee, editor.
Title: Marketing and outreach for the academic library : new approaches and initiatives / edited by
Bradford Lee Eden.
Description: Lanham : Rowman & Littlefield, [2016] | Series: Creating the 21st-century academic
library ; 7 | Includes bibliographical references and index.
Identifiers: LCCN 2016000813 (print) | LCCN 2016013058 (ebook) | ISBN 9781442262539 (cloth :
alk. paper) | ISBN 9781442262546 (pbk. : alk. paper) | ISBN 9781442262553 (electronic)
Subjects: LCSH: Academic libraries–Marketing. | Academic libraries–Public relations. | Library
outreach programs. | Academic libraries–Case studies.
Classification: LCC Z716.3 .M283 2016 (print) | LCC Z716.3 (ebook) | DDC 025.1/977–dc23 LC
record available at http://lccn.loc.gov/2016000813

Printed in the United States of America

Contents

Introduction

Volume 7 of the series Creating the 21st-Century Academic Library is focused on new approaches and initiatives in marketing the academic library, as well as the importance of outreach through partnerships and collaborations both internal and external to the library. The primary topics in this book are: implementation of social media strategies, the use of library spaces for collaboration and inspiration, planning events and extravaganzas in the library, librarians as coordinators of events and user-centered programming, the delivery of library services through digital engagement, using Instagram to create a library character for the YouTube generation, using workshops to promote digital library services, an examination of the new librarianship paradigm, the process of marketing and constructing a digital collection based on U.S. Highway 89 and the Intermountain West, and how librarians at Loyola University New Orleans have embedded their expertise and practice into their university culture.

Kaela Casey and Laura Worden begin this volume by describing their experiences implementing social media outreach at California State University, Channel Islands. A strong social media presence and strategy by the university itself presented opportunities for partnership and collaboration for successful engagement with library patrons. Working with university leadership, the library was able to construct a social media plan along with continual assessment options. Casey and Worden provide information on successes, challenges, and disappointments during the whole process, something that will be of great interest to those who are employing social media as part of their outreach strategy in their library.

Susan Van Alstyne elaborates on the development of various library space initiatives at the Berkeley College campus in Newark, New Jersey. One of nine campuses in the system, she describes ways that each campus library in the system has designed spaces for their various constituencies and how the Newark campus library has focused on its specific commuter clientele by working with the Student Library Advisory Council (SLAC) for ideas and with the athletic department, along with various clubs and student organizations. In the end, engagement with students and the local community has made the library a creativity center.

Karen Evans describes the evolution of the Library Extravaganza in the Cunningham Library at Indiana State University. This annual fall event, begun in 2001, has grown through campus and community support to become a major introduction to the new school year by the university, along with being an incredible marketing opportunity for the library. Free goody bags, free pizza and popcorn, and a scavenger hunt focused on library resources and study assistance have proven a huge draw for the students at the start of the fall semester. Evans also describes the development of an Events Center in the library, and how both the extravaganza and the center help the library to showcase its importance and relevance to university administration, faculty, and students.

Programming in academic libraries is the focus of Joe C. Clark's contribution on various outreach activities by Kent State University's Performing Arts Library. Examples include Welcome Week, Student Appreciation Day, the annual Open House, receptions for the Porthouse Academy and Kent/Blossom Music summer programs, along with Open Mic Lunch, The Director Speaks, the Colloquium series, Performing Arts *Live*, and Jazz Café. Each of these events is described in detail, along with a short list of benefits these events bring to the Performing Arts Library.

Kathryn Barwick and Mylee Joseph discuss various online communities developed by the State Library in New South Wales, Australia. Social media is used to market and promote library events, promote discovery of library assets, engage with clients and communities, and collect social media content and social metadata. Library working groups went through a two-year process to explore and evaluate various social media tools for their effectiveness in delivering library services and collections. Various digital engagement activities are described, and the library's investment and success in various initiatives provide an interesting example for other libraries whose clientele and communities are spread out over a wide geographic area.

The librarians at Albert S. Cook Library at Towson University detail their experiences with creating informative yet humorous library-related public service videos. Their attempts working with student actors, puppets, scripting, and technology exhibit great initiative and creativity, and is must-reading for anyone trying to do similar experiments producing YouTube videos for library marketing and outreach.

Tracy C. Bergstrom and Alexander Papson reflect on their experiences providing digital library workshops through the Center for Digital Scholarship at Notre Dame University. They describe staffing requirements, guidelines for workshop development, the results of workshop attendance in 2013–2014, lessons learned, and partnerships and collaborations under development for future workshops. The importance of word-of-mouth recommendations became a key component for future workshop programming.

Rebecca Parker and Dana McKay provide an extended opinion piece related to the future of librarianship as a profession. They describe three occupations that incorporate aspects of librarianship: business analysis, enterprise architecture, and knowledge management. Changes in the physical spaces within libraries, the importance of human computer interaction, and information openness and open access are other topics of discussion. In the end, the authors indicate that complacency is the enemy of librarianship more than anything else, and that new skill sets and new ideas along with a user-centered focus are the best attributes for the library profession going forward.

Finally, Maria Willey et al. detail their experiences with embedded librarianship at Loyola University, New Orleans. This includes library instruction, the Historical Methods lab, the University Honors Program, Introduction to Music Industry Studies class, and the Synoptic Gospels class.

Brad Cole and his colleagues document the process of selecting, digitizing, and marketing a unique digital collection based on Highway 89 in the western United States. They discuss the selection of a content management system, collaborative partners, metadata standards, marketing, and the many challenges of coordinating multiple participants.

It is hoped that this volume, and the series in general, will be a valuable and exciting addition to the discussions and planning surrounding the future directions, services, and careers in the twenty-first-century academic library.

Chapter One

Making Social Media Worth It

Planning and Implementing for a Small Institution

Kaela Casey and Laura Worden

Social media: what are they, how do libraries use the various services, and which are the best fit? Are librarians able to make the time commitment of social media while still handling all their other duties? And in the end, is it worth it? Despite the proliferation and popularity of social media, many libraries face these questions. Two librarians at John Spoor Broome Library at California State University Channel Islands (CI) recently faced them as they tried to find a direction for their social media outreach.

CI opened in 2002 with five hundred transfer students and several hundred extended education students from California State University Northridge. The library itself consisted of a two-thousand-square-foot building run by a library assistant and a small group of student assistants. By 2007–2008 the campus enrollment had reached 3,348, the library staff had grown to include eight librarians, and the library had moved to a new building of one hundred thirty-seven thousand square feet. During this time of growth, the Outreach Librarian looked to social media sites as a new way to reach out to students; however the endeavor was slowed due to workload, the move to the new building, and finally fate.

ANALYSIS

Broome Library's social media efforts were previously led by the outreach librarian with the assistance of the library's Social Media Team. In late 2012, the outreach librarian departed and the Social Media Team, a group composed of library staff and faculty from different areas, stopped meeting. In

August 2013, the authors were tasked with taking over management of Broome Library's social media presence. Both authors, as members of the team, contributed to conversations on the direction of the library's social media but were not in a position to make any decisions. Before stepping into the role of social media managers, the authors researched best practices for social media in academic libraries. They then analyzed Broome Library's current efforts in order to take steps to revitalize their presence.

There is a wealth of literature on the basics, benefits, and guidelines for social media planning and implementation for libraries. Many academic libraries utilize social media sites and consider them to be beneficial in reaching out to their student population (Chu and Du, 2012, pp. 68–70; Murphy and Meyer, 2013, p. 14). Information delivered immediately reaches students that have connected with the library through the sites, and the voice, tone, and message delivered allows the library to connect with students on a more personal level. Phillips (2011, p. 520) found that Facebook in particular allows libraries "to present themselves as approachable, in order to develop a rapport with students, which could ultimately facilitate the delivery of service." Despite these perceived benefits, libraries utilizing social media sites report difficulties in attracting a large audience and challenges with maintaining the sites due to time constraints or lack of staff with training and experience in social media (Chu and Du, 2012, pp. 70–71; Wan, 2010, p. 317). The ever-changing nature of social media presents an additional challenge to libraries. Social media sites wax and wane in popularity, new sites will pop up, and what works now may not work in the future (Solomon, 2011, p. 1). Nevertheless, it is recognized that social media are here to stay and have the potential to increase student awareness, engagement, and use of library services and resources. For that reason, a flexible, sustainable strategic plan for social media is necessary to focus limited staff time and resources to gain the maximum benefit (Steiner, 2012, pp. 6–7). With information from the literature in mind, the authors began analyzing the library's current social media presence.

As of August 2013, Broome Library had profiles on Facebook, Instagram, YouTube, and Flickr. Flickr had been well-managed by Unique Collections faculty and staff for several years, and they, as well as the authors, agreed it would remain under their auspices. The Instagram profile was created in November 2012 to post pictures of a specific campus event and garnered fifty-six followers. After that event, however, no new images were added and no plan was created to maintain the profile, leaving it stagnant. Broome Library had three YouTube accounts set up by three different library staff and faculty. Each person was unaware of the existence of other accounts and created their account to post one or two videos. The three accounts had no activity beyond the initial posts. Broome Library's Facebook page was the most active social media site and was set up with the assistance of the campus Information Technology department in 2009. At the time, eight library faculty and staff had administrator access to the Facebook profile, meaning they all could post content and interact with users on the page. Since no one was officially in charge of the page and no formal procedures or policies were established, the posts were sporadic and lacked a cohesive tone. While the page received a fair amount of likes, growth stalled and engagement with users through comments, shares, and posts was scarce.

The authors knew the campus's social media presence was strong, well-coordinated, and growing and changing to respond to the needs and interests of the student population. They looked into the campus efforts and discovered the campus social media sites were managed by the multimedia coordinator in the Communications and Marketing department. The multimedia coordinator had plans, timelines, and workflows to manage several social media sites for the campus, and actively assessed their efforts in order to make changes and improvements. As a result, the campus social media presence was active and flourishing with regular postings, a consistent voice and message, and active engagement with the student population across several platforms including Facebook, Instagram, Twitter, and Tumblr.

After the review, it was clear that a lack of leadership and written strategic plans, timelines, and procedures had resulted in an inconsistent social media presence for the library that was not reaching the student population effectively. The authors recognized the need to develop a social media strategic plan that combined elements from best practices described in the literature with successful strategies used by the campus social media presence. Like the libraries described in the literature, however, the authors had limited time and other duties in addition to managing social media, so any social media plans had to be practical and sustainable.

MAKING THE PLAN

To gain insight and guidance on developing a plan, the authors reached out to the campus multimedia coordinator. Both parties met and the multimedia coordinator offered practical advice, technical assistance, and ways to work together to enhance both parties' social media presence. He posed important questions to the authors: what do you want your audience to know, and how do you want to achieve that? He advised the authors to set goals, become part of the campus conversation by following other campus social media sites, and be as active as possible on all sites. In order to make the process of maintaining multiple sites easier, he also encouraged the authors to utilize a Wi-Fi-enabled iPad. This would allow them to access sites and post content from anywhere on campus. Since the campus social media sites already had a strong presence and following, the multimedia coordinator suggested sharing access to some sites. Instead of trying to revive the library's stagnant Instagram profile, he instead granted the authors access to the campus profile. This would allow the authors to easily reach a large audience and remove the burden of having an additional social media profile to maintain. Additionally, the multimedia coordinator had administrator access to the library's Facebook page so he could aid in monitoring any activity. This meeting not only cemented the relationship between the library and the multimedia coordinator, but also aided in clarifying what needed to be addressed in the library's social media plan.

It was essential for the library's social media plan to clearly articulate the overarching goals of the library's social media presence, a timeline for implementation, goals, best practices, procedures, plans for the future, and methods of evaluating the success of each profile. The authors also agreed, after careful consideration, to limit access to all the library social media sites to themselves and the multimedia coordinator. This would ensure consistency in the library's voice and message. The success or failure of the plan hinged on not overextending the library's resources, starting with a manageable amount of social media sites, and having a plan for future growth.

The overall goal was to establish a strong presence over multiple social media sites to allow Broome Library to educate its audience on library services, resources, and events; engage its audience in meaningful discussion; and empower its audience to access and utilize library services and resources. The plan identified target audiences: the campus community; prospective students; local community members, businesses, and organizations; and other libraries, museums, and cultural institutions. An additional component of the plan was an implementation timeline. The timeline defined the steps that needed to be taken before moving on to new social media efforts. It included critical tasks such as developing posting schedules and reestablishing the Social Media Team.

With the foundation of the plan in place, the authors moved on to delineating the specifics for Facebook and Instagram. The overarching social media goals were modified into individual goals that fit each site. Then best practices, procedures, and measurements for success were outlined. For Facebook, best practices focused on status updates, posting of images, writing style, tagging people, use of links in a post, how to respond to comments, and liking other pages. (See figure 1.1.)

Best practices for Instagram focused on image content, use of hashtags, sharing images to other social media sites, and writing style for the text accompanying images. Procedures were developed for others in the library to request content to be posted on either Facebook or Instagram to make the process easy and transparent. Finally, the authors set parameters for evaluating the outcome of the changes they were making. For both, this included looking at the number of post likes, shares, and comments. Additionally for

---

FACEBOOK

GOALS
1. Promote library services, resources, and events;
2. Interact with students, staff, faculty, and community members; and
3. Provide students, staff, faculty, and community members with a public forum for asking questions and providing feedback.

BEST PRACTICES

STATUS UPDATES
- Include a photo/image when possible
    - If creating an image, size should be 504 pixels wide
- For text:
    - Keep it brief and to the point
    - Use a friendly, natural tone that shows a real person is posting
    - Double-check your text for spelling and grammatical errors
- Include any people/pages you want tagged in the post
- Include any links you want in the post
    - Use https://bitly.com/ to shorten your URL
- Incorporate images/concepts from popular culture if relevant/possible
    - For example, look at popular memes (check www.knowyourmeme.com), think about current popular TV shows or movies, etc.
- Keep in mind - How does this benefit the library? What is the payoff for the reader?

Figure 1.1. Goals and best practices for Facebook taken from Broome Library's Social Media Plan

Facebook, they planned to track the number of overall page likes to note any change.

The final step in the process was to reestablish the library's Social Media Team. Having been a part of the original team, the authors knew soliciting feedback and ideas from others would benefit their efforts. Library faculty and staff were selected from various areas to provide wide-ranging ideas on the library's social media needs. The team reviewed the existing social media efforts and the authors' social media plan, best practices, and procedures. The team provided feedback on the plan, offered ideas on how each of their areas could contribute content, and discussed plans for the future. With a plan and team in place, the authors were ready to move forward.

IMPLEMENTING THE PLAN

As a first step, the authors met with the Social Media Team to select content to post to Facebook. Members of the team were able to provide information on events and exhibits in the library, new resources and services from their areas, and ideas for content they had gathered from student feedback, such as posting staff profiles to familiarize the students with their librarians and library staff. With content selected, the authors set up a paper and online calendar they then shared with team members. Initially, the paper calendar was to be a "draft" calendar that could be easily changed, while the online calendar was to be the "official" social media calendar. The calendars were used to schedule reminders for creating and posting content for Facebook and taking photographs for Instagram. Since the calendars were shared, team members were able to make updates and add information, such as noting that an event was canceled or that a new digital collection would be made available on a certain date.

Although the Social Media Team members were likely to have inside knowledge on content that should be posted to the library's social media sites, the authors were aware that other library faculty and staff might also have things they would like to contribute. Consequently, the authors informed all library faculty and staff of the newly developed social media plan, introduced them to the library's Facebook page and the campus's Instagram page, and advised them on how to request a social media post. Library faculty and staff found this helpful because they were now aware of all social media outlets available to them and knew the process to follow to get something posted.

To create content effectively, the authors looked into standard image sizes for Facebook, created templates using Adobe Photoshop, and downloaded photo-collage-making apps to the social media iPad. They used these templates and apps to create engaging graphics that highlighted areas of the library and campus, and drew from popular culture memes and trends among the student population. When possible, the graphics created included text in order to get the message across quickly and limit the amount of descriptive text. (See figure 1.2.)

Following the social media calendar, the authors created a semester's worth of social media content. The initial postings were the traditional start-of-the-semester welcome back, library hours, and upcoming holidays. The circulation coordinator was the first to submit a request to post what identification students needed to check out library items. The request included an image, text, and the date to post. The authors took advantage of the post-scheduling option in Facebook, and scheduled all posts in advance.

Much of the content that would be posted to Instagram could not be created in advance; therefore, the authors trained members of the Social Media Team on using the iPad to take photos, create collages, and post images to Instagram. Available members of the team were then scheduled to be present and photograph events in the library. Very quickly, the authors found that many things that would be fun and appropriate to post to Instagram were not necessarily scheduled events. For example, images of student clubs recruiting in front of the library or new additions to the library such as a

Figure 1.2. Example of Facebook post

phone-charging station were popular posts. Since the entire library staff was aware of the Instagram profile, the authors or members of the team were notified whenever something of interest was seen. Having multiple people with access and the ability to use the iPad, made it possible to capture and post images at a moment's notice.

After the first semester, the authors felt comfortable with the initial implementation and they began to move forward with expanding the library's social media presence to Pinterest. With input from the team, best practices and procedures were developed and seven initial boards were selected for creation: a shared "What Are You Reading?" board, What's New at Broome, Archives and Digital Collections, Library Events, Library Displays and Exhibits, New Books, and New Movies. (See figure 1.3.)

The boards were first created as secret boards and were populated with images that linked back to pertinent websites like the library catalog or event web pages. Working with members of the Social Media Team was imperative, as some members were the only ones with knowledge of and access to relevant content. For example, the library's Cataloging and Acquisitions staff member received all new books and movies; therefore, she was able to inform the authors of upcoming titles to post. Once the initial boards were populated with seven to ten pins, the boards were made public. After launching Pinterest, members of the Social Media Team continued to submit content to post and the authors created new boards to coincide with upcoming events, such as Banned Books Week. To keep the impact on workload low, the authors decided to pin new content to existing boards every two weeks and create new boards to promote larger events and celebrations as needed.

Although the authors had planned to move forward with YouTube after Pinterest, they had to make a change in plans after being approached by the

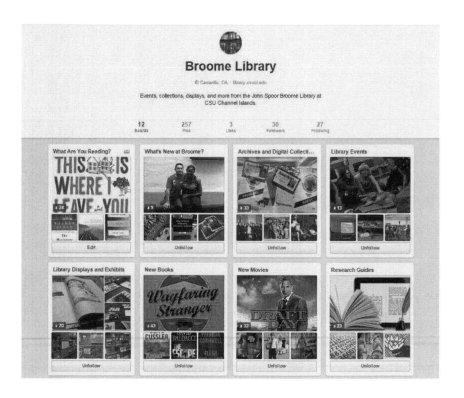

Figure 1.3.   Broome Library's Pinterest page. Retrieved from https://www.pinterest.com/broomelibrary/

campus multimedia coordinator. The authors discovered CI would be launching a campus-specific social media site called CampusQuad. (See figure 1.4.)

The multimedia coordinator set the authors up with accounts and provided training. CampusQuad was similar to Instagram, in that the site supported the posting of images with a limited amount of text. Therefore, the policies and procedures associated with CampusQuad were adapted from the already-created Instagram policies and procedures. CampusQuad was then introduced to the Social Media Team and reminders were added to the social media calendar.

EVALUATING THE EFFORT

There are many ways to gauge the effectiveness of social media efforts, from feedback to evaluating data to personal reflection. In their planning, the authors developed overarching goals for the library's social media, as well as specific goals for each site. These goals touched on promotion of the library and engagement with the campus community and, for Facebook, included specific targets for likes, comments, and shares. The authors received positive feedback from library faculty and staff who felt the revived social media efforts were of value to the library. Students also expressed excitement at the library's increased presence, and enjoyed posing for photos that would be used on the various sites. Additionally, library administration felt the efforts were beneficial and supported the hiring of a student assistant to aid the authors' work. In addition to considering the anecdotal evidence and the potential of having a student assistant, the authors looked at the data available to ascertain what goals were met, reflected on the positives and negatives of the experience, and determined the next steps.

Instagram, CampusQuad, and Pinterest do not provide any canned statistical analyses of page performance; therefore, the authors looked at the number of likes, comments, followers, or re-pins. Using the campus Instagram profile proved to be successful, as the profile has over twenty-seven hundred followers, and images posted by the authors consistently received more than one hundred fifty likes and numerous comments from followers. The authors only posted to CampusQuad a few times and did not get any likes or comments. Despite this, the authors decided to continue to post to the profile because the site is still being promoted to the campus community and has the potential to grow. The library's Pinterest profile has gotten more than thirty followers and about forty user re-pins of library content. Additionally, the shared board has a total of twenty-two pins from seven unique users. Although usage appears low on Pinterest, it is possible that users without Pinterest accounts are viewing the profile and individual boards. Due to this and the low impact on staff time, the authors felt it would be beneficial to contin-

Figure 1.4. Screenshot of library events posted to CampusQuad

ue their efforts with Pinterest and reevaluate at a later date. The addition of a student assistant will be helpful in getting more photos of events and students around the library and providing even more updates to these sites.

Facebook page administrators can access detailed statistics and data on page performance from the Insights tab. Under this tab, page administrators can access data that gives an overview of page likes, post reach, user visits, and engagement. Administrators can also download a detailed Insights Data Report on page data, post data, or video data. The authors monitored the Insights tab regularly and when they were ready to take a more comprehensive look at their efforts downloaded an Insights Data Report. While the authors found the page overviews given under the Insights tab helpful and easy to understand, they found the Insights Data Report cumbersome and confusing. The authors again reached out to the multimedia coordinator, who was able to prepare a brief data report for them and also directed them to try the free website LikeAlyzer (www.likealyzer.com) to obtain clear and concise information and recommendations to improve page performance.

Using information from the Insights tab, the report prepared by the multimedia coordinator, and information gained from LikeAlyzer, the authors took a more in-depth look at their use of Facebook. The authors found that from August 2013 to August 2014, the library's Facebook page had more than one hundred new page likes, individual post reach had increased from an average of forty-six to eighty-one people, and the page's total reach (which includes post reach, comments, likes, shares, and other page activity) increased from an average of 186 to 560 people (Facebook, 2015). (See figure 1.5.)

Likes, comments, and shares for individual posts rose from an average of one to seven (Meltwater, 2015). From observation of page activity, the authors noticed that those liking the page, making comments, and sharing posts were increasingly members of the campus community. Despite the increases in statistics, the authors did not reach all of the goals and target numbers they had set for the page in the social media plan.

The authors set eight hundred as the target for the number of page likes and fell short by about fifty likes; however, the page's total reach surpassed the target of five hundred people. The number of likes, comments, and shares on individual posts occasionally reached the target number of more than twenty. The authors observed that posts on popular library events, such as a therapy dog day during finals week, and important information for students, like days the library would be closed, received the most likes, comments, and shares. Although there was more engagement via likes, comments, and shares, the authors did not observe or engage in any discussion with students through Facebook. Students occasionally made comments or asked a question; however, it never evolved into a dialogue between the library and students.

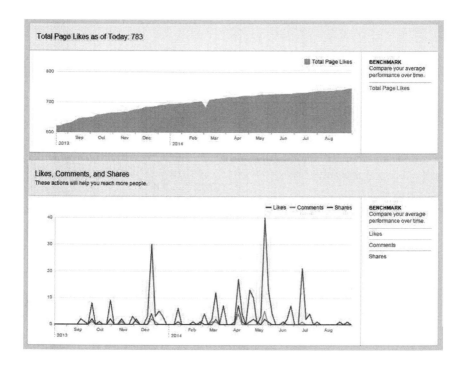

Figure 1.5.   Total page likes and likes, comments, and shares from Broome Library's Facebook Insights

Although improvements were seen in the library's Facebook presence, they were not as marked as the authors had hoped. The report from LikeAlyzer also noted areas that could be improved to enhance the library's page, including adding Milestones, posting between peak usage hours, using hashtags, and asking more questions of the audience. Implementing these changes were simple, and the authors made them immediately. For the future, the authors will continue to monitor statistics and get reports from LikeAlyzer in order to improve page performance. With a student assistant to create content, promote the page, and provide a fresh look at what his or her peers enjoy and want out of Facebook, the authors foresee even more improvement.

While looking at the statistics and goals helped to point out areas of success and those for improvement in regards to page performance, the authors also reflected on the day-to-day logistics of the new social media plan to determine what worked and what did not. The authors felt the most successful change to the library's social media process was the use and sharing of the paper calendar. The authors kept the calendar up-to-date by inputting important dates and events based on their meetings with the Social Media Team and by posting requests from library faculty and staff. Library faculty and staff also input events or important dates they were aware of to keep the authors informed. The monthly print calendar allowed the authors to visualize the most effective posting schedule for the month, ensure they were consistently posting to all sites, preschedule postings on Facebook, and utilize their time more efficiently.

Limiting access to profiles and communicating the social media plan and processes to all library faculty and staff also alleviated many of the previous problems encountered. With clear communication, library faculty and staff understood that the authors were the primary managers of the sites and knew the process to request something be posted on their behalf. Since only the authors could access and authorize access to profiles, consistency was maintained. Social media best practices were followed, sites were posted to on a regular basis, and the authors developed the tone and voice of the library's presence.

Reaching out to the campus's social media experts also proved to be invaluable. The authors gained greater insight and knowledge on social media technology and best practices, and formed an ongoing collaboration with the campus multimedia coordinator. With the aid of the multimedia coordinator, the authors set up and began using iPads to maintain the library's social media sites. The portability of the iPads meant the authors could access social media apps and other third-party apps to create and post content quickly and efficiently. Additionally, sharing access and connecting to other campus areas' social media sites allowed the library to capitalize on existing audiences, share information, and join in on campus conversations.

Although the authors felt their efforts were successful, there were some disappointments and areas for improvement. Tracking events and important dates and scheduling postings ahead of time was essential to keeping things organized; however, maintaining two calendars was not. Initially, the authors used a print and online calendar, both of which were shared with the Social Media Team. It proved to be confusing and the authors tended to prefer the print calendar and neglected the online. The authors decided to abandon use of the online calendar and continue to maintain a print calendar. Obtaining photos of events, exhibits, and students in the library was also a great challenge. Since events could take place day or night, any day of the week, they were not able to attend every event. Asking members of the Social Media Team proved difficult as well because of workload and availability. The authors hope this problem will be alleviated in the future with the hiring of a student assistant and will continue to schedule themselves or members of the Social Media Team as they are available.

In taking a look at the successes, challenges, and disappointments of their efforts, the authors believed the investment in social media planning and implementation was worthwhile. The library now has an expanded social media presence. Goals, best practices, and processes are outlined for each site, profiles are regularly updated, and the library has a consistent voice and message. Data and statistics gathered from the sites show a slow but steady improvement in each page's performance and engagement. The authors identified ways to fine-tune their social media plan and processes and integrate a student assistant into their team. In addition to being able to delegate tasks to a student assistant, the authors will now have a student voice to aid them in their overall planning.

CONCLUSION

At the start of this endeavor, the authors had some social media knowledge and limited time to spend dedicated to social media. They discovered the benefits and challenges libraries encounter when implementing social media and sought ways to maximize the benefits and preemptively address the challenges. Key to their success was reaching out and collaborating with on-campus social media experts and getting buy-in and participation from library faculty and staff. They then were able to draft and implement a detailed strategic social media plan with procedures, guidelines, timelines, and workflows. This plan was followed and Broome Library saw increased engagement on Facebook, became active on Instagram, and launched new social media profiles on Pinterest and CampusQuad. By investing time in researching, creating, and implementing a strategic social media plan, the authors have ensured their library will continue to maintain and grow its presence in order to reach their student population effectively while making a minimal impact on staff time.

HELPFUL RESOURCES

BitLy (https://bitly.com/): This website will shorten URLs. The authors use this site to create short URLs to place in Facebook posts.

Know Your Meme (http://knowyourmeme.com/): This website contains information on current Internet memes and viral media. The authors use this to stay up-to-date on current social media trends.

LikeAlyzer by Meltwater (http://likealyzer.com/): This website will analyze your Facebook page and provide statistics and recommendations for improvement.

LiPix: This free app, available on the iTunes store, allows users to edit photos and create collages for Instagram. There is a "pro" version for a fee.

Mashable (http://mashable.com/): This website contains news, information, and resources on technology trends and social media.

PicMonkey (http://www.picmonkey.com/): This website allows users to edit photos and create collages in various sizes. Most content is free; users can upgrade to access more content.

REFERENCES

Chu, S. K., and H. S. Du. 2012. "Social Networking Tools for Academic Libraries." *Journal of Librarianship and Information Science* 45: 64–75. doi: 10.1177/0961000611434361.

Facebook. 2015. *Insights* [data file]. Retrieved from https://www.facebook.com/BroomeLibrary/insights/.

Meltwater. 2015. *LikeAlyzer: Review of John Spoor Broome Library CSUCI.* http://likealyzer.com/facebook/broomelibrary.

Murphy, J., and H. Meyer. 2013. "Best (and Not So Best) Practices in Social Media." *ILA Reporter* 31: 12–15.

Phillips, N. K. 2011. "Academic Library Use of Facebook: Building Relationships with Students." *Journal of Academic Librarianship* 37 (6): 512–22. doi: 10.1016/j.acalib.2011.07.008.

Solomon, L. 2011. *Doing Social Media So It Matters: A Librarian's Guide.* Chicago: American Library Association.

Steiner, S. K. 2012. *Strategic Planning for Social Media in Libraries.* Chicago: American Library Association.

Wan, G. 2010. "How Academic Libraries Reach Users on Facebook." *College & Undergraduate Libraries* 18: 307–18. doi: 10.1080/10691316.2011.624944.

Chapter Two

Library Spaces

Inspiration and Collaboration

Susan Van Alstyne

Providing a space conducive to study, research, and student success is one of the many goals of an academic library. Over the past five years, the Newark, New Jersey, campus library at Berkeley College has evolved to encourage creative interaction. The library strives to provide an educational space where students not only come to learn, but also to encourage participatory learning. At the same time, the librarians learn how to provide the spaces and services students need. The importance of library design and meeting spaces along with librarian assistance has increased the use of resources. Student organizations from the fashion club to the Student Library Advisory Council (SLAC) use the library meeting rooms in addition to using the main library on a regular basis. Providing a space furnished with moveable tables and chairs and equipped with the latest technology has increased the use of the meeting rooms and library resources overall. To accommodate student needs the library completed two expansion projects within two years. The successful use of the library space is an example of what is possible with minimal staff and resources.

Berkeley College has nine campus libraries located in different cities within the New York/New Jersey metropolitan area (Berkeley College, 2015). Although the campus libraries have consistent circulation policies to ensure students have the same experience at each campus, students' needs differ from campus to campus depending on the student population. Several of the Berkeley College campus libraries have had and continue to have much success with programs similar to what one can find in public libraries, such as poetry reading events. As the Newark campus library has seen, student support departments such as career services and faculty collaboration are essential to providing successful programs. Not all programs work well at all campuses, however, or garner the same interest and feedback. The Paramus, New Jersey, campus has had success with play adaptations such as *A Midsummer Night's Dream*. Associates from several departments, faculty, and fashion students were involved in creating a well-attended production, leaving the campus community wanting more. The staff recognizes the Newark students would benefit from such a production; however, the Newark campus library has considerably more circulation where small programs are useful, but the space and student needs differ greatly. Laptop, netbook, and course textbook circulation statistics are consistently higher than the other New Jersey campuses. The Berkeley College Newark campus's diverse population of students may have limited or no access to technology and need to maximize their time on campus balancing work and family responsibilities.

EVOLUTION OF SPACE AND USE

The academic library has always, at least in the librarian's view, been the heart of the campus—the center of ideas! Open any publication, and there is no lack of articles about libraries' imminent demise. There is a glimmer of hope, however, where many libraries are maximizing their spaces with innovative designs and implementing programs to provide services—from makerspaces to business incubators and collaborative spaces. Over the last thirty-plus years, as technology integrated with education changed how students and educators use technology, libraries had to adapt and embrace this change in education. In the literature, many librarians consult with anthropologists, architects, interior designers, and information technology professionals in order to adapt to this dynamic, where the space is designed toward how technology is being used. Academic libraries are designing more group workspaces and adding more technology to cater to students bringing their own devices as well as providing technological tools to lend to students. When designing the twenty-first-century library, it is crucial to be able to respond to the needs of all users. While this merging of physical and virtual worlds is a wonderful time for libraries, since the library remains the space for learning and research, it is also necessary to accommodate the needs of the population (Bell and Shank, 2007). Compliance with the Americans with Disabilities Act (ADA) as well as technology that enables one to supply transcripts to video lectures are necessary; the space needs to be supportive of the special needs of the population. In addition to complying with ADA and remaining cognizant of the different learning styles and needs of the population—some prefer working alone in a quiet environment while others prefer a more interactive atmosphere working in groups—it is important to recognize the students with invisible needs (ACRL, 2014). Over the past six years, librarians have worked with several students with challenges who now have become daily library visitors.

Creating library spaces to encourage interaction and collaboration is a necessity. Why is this important? The library needs to maintain its role within the institution by contributing to the enrichment of campus life while quantifying its value to all stakeholders. The library is the crux of the social and academic world; the twenty-first-century library provides a place for students to study, relax, collaborate, and yes—snack! The library has evolved into an amalgamation of public spaces for engagement using interactive technology. There are many debates that libraries are not community centers— why not? Libraries have always been at the heart of serving the community—whether it be urban city, suburbia, or academic large and small.

Creating a student-centered library is about building connections and combining the physical and virtual worlds. Library space and budgets restrict what is possible, but the concepts are applicable from the smallest college to the largest university. Berkeley College Newark campus library users are accessing library resources physically and virtually using a variety of tools including smartphones, tablets, and laptops in addition to desktops. Today's librarians are agile in supporting their users when needed, both figuratively and physically, with online collaborative platforms and on-site spaces. Just as instructors create learning environments in the classroom, librarians are doing the same when creating collaborative spaces to enhance the student experience.

Learning commons, information commons, academic commons! Many institutions are using this term to describe the convergence of social and learning spaces and services. Due to the small library space at each campus library at Berkeley College, library services are combined—there is no separate circulation and reference area. All the on-site checkouts and reference services happen at the circulation desk. The five libraries featured in the July 2012 issue of *Library Journal* provide inspiration for all sizes of libraries considering a renovation (Schaper, 2012, p. 20). Although the library redesign budgets are out of reach for some, the article provides some ideas on the common theme of supporting collaborative spaces to encourage participatory learning and creating experiences.

Inspirational artwork and educational displays are an important element in creating experiences. Keeping things new is an important part of library design when there is no budget to renovate or repair areas that affect workflow such as the circulation desk. Changing displays is an inexpensive method of keeping things fresh. A good shopping trip to a retail store always provides some inspiration. One example from 2009 is when the Newark campus library started using a digital frame at the circulation desk after observing how a hair salon used a digital frame to market events and specials at the salon. The very next week, the library director purchased a $40 digital

frame, then loaded it with a visually appealing PowerPoint with library information, and used this at the circulation desk to share information with students. Many students stopped to read the display and automatically started to
touch the screen and provide unsolicited feedback: usually the most honest
and best feedback of all. Students were looking for touch screen components
in the library. Indirect and direct data collection methods in evaluating the
user experience have helped in the library's project-planning process.

LIBRARY AS ECOSYSTEM

When expanding Berkeley College Newark library, the librarians had to take
a holistic view of the library. As the budget allowed, a few items considered
included sound, lighting, furniture, shelving options, collections, security,
signage, and technology. Sustainable building design is a significant factor
when redesigning a library. The library provides the essentials: computer
workstations, Wi-Fi access printing and copying service, and study spaces.
The librarian of the future needs to embody the soul of the architect, designer, sociologist, and anthropologist. Just as homes are a place for memories,
libraries provide transformative spaces during the transformative years of the
lives of students.

As an academic library in an urban setting, many of Berkeley College's
students have access to local public libraries in Newark or cities where they
live. The librarians encourage the use of local libraries and museums all the
time. When the library staff suggests to students to use the public library
across the street from the college, the immediate reaction from the majority
of the students is, "That place needs a facelift. It is so dark, old and depress-
ing." When meeting new students entering the library for the first time, many
come with these ingrained misconceptions about the library. As librarians,
the goal is to support and promote student success while providing optimal
physical and virtual environments catering to today's 24/7 culture.

SERENDIPITY

The spaces at the Newark campus library provide opportunities for the students and in larger part the campus communities. Library managers need to
be visionaries when planning expansion projects. The experience of this
relatively small library is applicable to even larger institutions—the ideals
and the motions of planning are the same, minus a few zeros off the budget.
When the campus library opened in 2007, the library occupied a small space
in the lower level of the building. After observing how students used the
library and how the library was at full capacity at several intervals during the
day, it was decided that the expansion was needed. Within two years, the

library was moved to the first floor of the building and to a larger space—and remained the center of the campus. Simultaneously the collection has doubled to more than ten thousand books and DVDs.

The campus, with less than five hundred students, is comprised primarily of commuter students—both fresh from high school and adult learners returning to school after changing careers and raising families. In comparison to all the other campus libraries, the librarians observed that more students were spending more time in the library. Not only were they using social media on the PCs and laptops, but the students were using the new space to work on group projects. Gradually, many student clubs began to meet in the library. The library had modern seating, great lighting, and a stylish color pattern—all thanks to prudent decisions made by the vice president of library services. At the grand opening of the expanded library in 2009, many remarked about the beautiful color scheme, furniture, and layout, and they still do. On this commuter campus, the library is the only place that is "homey" and where students can relax. The library offers multipurpose game tables where students play chess when taking a break from their studies. Inside the library, there is a conference room available for use with moveable tables. There was much debate during the building process. Initially, the idea was to open the conference room for all campus staff to use for meetings, but there was no conclusion how to use this room effectively. Ultimately, the students decided how the room should be used! Without the conference room, the library would be "standing room only" during the day. Furthermore, it would be impossible to accommodate the students working on group projects. This room became a good practice area for students to use for public speaking classes, where they would practice privately and record their presentations. As the activity in the library kept increasing, the librarians recognized the need for additional group space. In order to support specific academic programs, it was proposed to build a law library, which was approved for the next fiscal year. At present, the law library is located directly across the hall from the main library. The law library is a much-coveted space, not only by the legal studies and criminal justice students accessing the justice collection, but also by student organizations ranging from the Student Government Association to the Fashion Club. Students change the room setup with moveable tables and chairs, use the projector and whiteboard for meetings, and share presentations. Staff and other administrators request the law library to hold meetings. Occasionally, the career counselor uses the room for mock interviews with students.

The library provides a nicely decorated space with moveable tables, rolling chairs, a computer workstation, projector, and dry-erase whiteboard. Even without a 3D printer, which would make an ideal addition, the library has provided a space that ignites students' creativity. The librarians even had a few impromptu database sessions on how to search fashion databases such as Stylesight (now WGSN). The students used the room to prepare for a local fashion show. The students were so grateful for the library providing the space that, following the fashion show, the students made a poster board to display in the library. The poster board provides biographical information about the students along with pictures and their design philosophies. The library proudly displayed it for close to a year. The library still has the poster board and displays the board from time to time. Fashion students created bookmarks with string and beads, and gave the librarians some to share and distribute with other students. Currently, the library does not have scheduling software to book the law library and conference room. As room use continues to increase, and in some cases a group of students will meet on a regular basis, librarians request students to schedule the room at the beginning of the quarter to reserve the law library.

After years of observing how students use the library, the library staff has learned that students need the space and freedom to create, thus improving their academic experience. A student's positive experience may contribute to student success and increased graduation rate. Even with the steady number of students at the campus from year to year, the library had to start using an empty classroom adjacent to the law library. After documenting increased room use, there is now a proposal to repurpose that empty classroom as a creative space for fashion students.

STUDENT LIBRARY ADVISORY COUNCIL (SLAC)

After observing how the students enjoyed coming to the library, the library director decided to create a Student Library Advisory Council (SLAC) on the Newark campus. The SLAC became a successful group with regular meetings and provided the library staff with some excellent feedback. To guide the librarians in the development phase, the librarians performed an online search and discovered many academic libraries have a student advisory council. The SLAC at Berkeley College Newark campus was modeled after the SLAC at the Berkeley College Brooklyn campus library. A page was created on the Newark Campus LibGuide to include the mission and objectives of the student organization. The mission: To ensure that the library is providing an inclusive environment with resources, facilities, and services conducive to student learning and success. The LibGuide also lists the objectives. SLAC is a student-run committee that meets regularly to discuss and seek resolution and improvement on all matters relating to the campus library. The library director consults with the committee chair or cochairs to develop agendas and schedule meetings. Council member activity may include (1) offering a student perspective on library issues, (2) developing and deploying awareness campaigns, (3) serving as library ambassadors during open houses, and

(4) eliciting periodic feedback from students through "hallway" mini surveys (Berkley College, n.d.).

At the very first SLAC meeting, students provided suggestions such as adding displays and signage similar to Barnes & Noble to allow browsing using subject headings, and changing the shelving location of the DVDs. The group mentioned they would be more inclined to join a book club to discuss nonfiction books focusing on self-improvement and business rather than fiction books. Suggestions included library workshops providing quick computer basics and database reviews and trips to the Newark Museum—all wonderful, low-cost doable suggestions provided by the group's very first meeting. With unknown expectations, it was a pure joy to hear how passionate the students were about the library. Each student took on a role, with one in charge of programming and another taking the lead with signage and design suggestions. The librarians listened to their suggestions and made some changes such as making DVDs more visible.

On three separate occasions, the librarians were able to escort students to the museum for free self-guided tours. The feedback was great! The students remarked that this was the first time visiting the museum. All this from students coming together and collaborating. The group also expressed interest in volunteering in the community. The initial group of students (who were in their third and fourth year) eventually moved on and graduated. A new group was formed, which had many suggestions for meet and greets, socials, and even a student appreciation day!

The library staff is helping to facilitate bringing their ideas to life. The students' suggestion to share movie reviews has been implemented. Although the catalog offers the feature to share reviews available via the online catalog, students did not use this feature. Rather, a low-tech approach was taken, where the students enjoyed reading the collected student review forms displayed in a binder at the circulation desk. The current SLAC members are working with the student government club to arrange volunteer opportunities in the area, and are seeking collaborative opportunities with other clubs and scheduling meetings in the library.

SCHOLAR ATHLETES

In 2011, the athletic director approached the library to arrange study hall for the basketball players. The library staff embraced this idea, where the athletes would sign in with the librarian, who would make arrangements with the tutoring center to ensure tutors would be available during the study sessions. The library offered time-management workshops and quick research tutorials in the library conference room before each study session. By the next week following the first "study hall," almost all of the athletes became library regulars. The athletes would come in and work individually, and also have group meetings in the library conference room. The athletes started to reserve the law library to use the projector to view plays before a game. Study sessions in addition to the time spent in the library helped the athletes academically, and with having an overall positive experience.

LIBRARY DEDICATION CEREMONY

On October 31, 2013, the Newark campus library was dedicated to Donald M. Payne Sr., born in Newark. He was the first African American congressman from New Jersey. Inspired by the educational and humanitarian legacy of Donald M. Payne Sr., the library experienced a "renaissance." Although distinguished members of the local and college community along with the media celebrated this occasion, no students were directly involved in the ceremony. Some students have knowledge of Donald M. Payne's legacy—one student even knew him personally. Sadly, at the time, the majority of students asked: "Who is this guy?" As the oil portrait awaited installation on the wall, the librarians took photographs with the students alongside the painting. The photographs were later developed with one of Donald M. Payne's quotes printed on the back: "Nothing is as powerful as a dream whose time has come." The dedication ceremony was a wonderful opportunity to support and encourage student involvement in governance, community, and history (Berkeley College, 2013).

EXTERNAL ENVIRONMENT

The Newark campus is within walking distance to a museum, library, and other cultural institutions. The library has developed relationships with these institutions to expose the students to their neighborhood. The displays in the library throughout the year aim to be educational. In 2014, New Jersey was celebrating "NJ350" (350 years of New Jersey history), and this was a wonderful time to display facts about Newark and New Jersey's history. The display engaged many students with some comments, including "I walk past that building [the New Jersey Historical Society] all the time—I had no idea . . . I did not know all this history in Newark." Popular culture references—mixing the past with the present—meet the students where the material is relevant to them. One successful display was "The Sports and the Arts" in February 2014. The Super Bowl was held in New Jersey in 2014, and the first Super Bowl trophy was made in Newark (Johnson, 2014). The library's display promoted the fact that the Newark Museum had the original Super Bowl trophy on display.

RESOURCES

The more students spend time in the library, the more attuned they become to the library collection. The Law and Justice Club holds weekly meetings in the law library, and the club president has made several book and DVD suggestions. Based on their recommendations, a DVD with public performance rights (PPRs) was purchased, which the club viewed and discussed during several meetings. The fashion club members use a projector and computer to share presentations and ideas. The fashion club is one of the most active clubs, with a large number of students, and is also active in the Newark community. The librarians create LibGuides that correspond with current activities and events on campus and keep the LibGuide on display using a Netbook where students can navigate to view more information. Library regulars have just formed an entrepreneurship club and have expressed interest in creating a business hub in the library. Recently, the librarians asked students to describe the library in one word in order to create a word cloud about the library. Although technically two words, "My Office" is one description that stands out.

CONCLUSION AND RECOMMENDATIONS

Innovative library design and meeting spaces along with librarian assistance has increased the use of resources, and solidified the library's importance within the campus community. As a library with minimal resources, the Newark campus library has successfully involved students with design and resource decisions. Encouraging creative interaction between student organizations by listening to the community, involving the community, and providing the space and resources to encourage creativity is key to the success of the twenty-first-century library. Librarians have evolved from the "keepers of books" to experience creators who hope to continue to inspire students' dreams.

REFERENCES

ACRL. 2014. *Academic Library Building Design: Resources for Planning*. Association of College and Research Libraries, October 22. http://wikis.ala.org/acrl/index.php/Academic_Library_Building_Design:_Resources_for_Planning.

Bell, S. J., and J. D. Shank. 2007. *Academic Librarianship by Design: A Blended Librarian's Guide to the Tools and Techniques*. Chicago: American Library Association.

Berkeley College. 2013. "Donald M. Payne Library Dedication." *LibGuides at Berkeley College*. Accessed February 1, 2015. http://berkeleycollege.libguides.com/DonaldMPayneLibrary.

———. 2015. "Welcome to Berkeley College." http://berkeleycollege.edu/home.htm.

———. n.d. "SLAC Newark Chapter." *LibGuides at Berkeley College*. Accessed February 1, 2015. http://berkeleycollege.libguides.com/newarklibrarySLAC.

Johnson, B. 2014. "Vince Lombardi Trophy Centerpieces 'City of Silver and Gold: From Tiffany to Cartier.'" Exhibit at Newark Museum. Accessed February 1, 2015. http://features. jerseyarts.com/content/index.php/nj-visual-arts/2014/01/vince-lombardi-trophy-centerpieces-city-of-silver-and-gold-from-tiffany-to-cartier-exhibit-at-newark-museum/.

NJ350. n.d. "What Is NJ350?" The Official New Jersey 350th Anniversary Website. Accessed February 1, 2015. http://officialnj350.com/what-is-nj350/.

Schaper, L. 2012. Standing Tall on Campus. *Library Journal* 137 (12): 20. http://search. proquest.com/docview/1022969644?accountid=38129.

Chapter Three

Events and Extravaganzas at Cunningham Memorial Library

Karen Evans

Indiana State University (ISU), established in 1865, is a public doctoral-granting institution, located in western Indiana (Hine, 2008). The campus, set on 435 acres, is home to the Cunningham Memorial Library, which bills itself as the campus living room to the enrolled 12,448 students. The library has five floors (two are below ground), with the basement and third floor deemed silent study floors. The first floor of the library houses the Public Services department, which includes the circulation, instructional technology, and reference desks. Plentiful seating, computer tables and carrels, along with a coffee shop, make the first floor a busy and often noisy area of the library. This floor is also the location for the Library Extravaganza and The Events Area, two well-known and unique resources that promote the library to the campus and the community.

THE LIBRARY EXTRAVAGANZA

The Library Extravaganza is an annual fall event to welcome students, staff, and faculty to the library and campus. Held on a Thursday in September, the one-day five-hour event draws hundreds of students, staff, and faculty to the library to enjoy pizza and learn about the resources available in the library and on campus.

The extravaganza started as a Welcome to the Library Fair in 2001, when a recently hired librarian asked the head of reference what the library did to welcome students to campus in the fall. The seminal idea of creating a welcome fair was conceived by the librarian, with an additional librarian and staff employee joining to create the planning team for the first welcome event. The event was envisioned as a way for students to meet faculty and staff and roam around the library to discover resources without the pressure of needing to find materials for an upcoming assignment. The dean of the library approved the plan, and offered a budget of $500 to plan the event and buy food and prizes. The event was scheduled for August 28 and 29 from 9 AM to noon with the theme of "Passport to the Library," because a main theme of the event was to highlight resources and materials in the library. The planning team hoped an international theme would promote the library's collection to American and international students. Decorations for the event included plastic globes of the world inflated and suspended from the ceiling. Flags from various countries and greetings written in numerous languages helped to create an international atmosphere for the event. Lunch-size brown bags were stamped with ISU Library and filled with candy, pencils, high-lighters, and bookmarks, tied with an ISU-colored blue ribbon and handed out to students from tables set up in the lobby of the library. Faculty and staff manned the tables, encouraging the students to take a gift bag, chips, cookies, and water, and to participate in prize drawings over the two-day event. To be eligible for prizes, students had to visit three floors of the library, view the displays in the showcases on the floors, and answer three questions about the displays. Fodor's tour guides, language resources, and foreign-country infor-mation were displayed in the showcases. Several drawings were held throughout the event, with the prizes varying from baskets filled with snacks and college necessities to coupons and gift certificates from the campus bookstore, salons, pizza restaurants, and video stores. With the small budget, the planning team had to be creative with the prizes. The team purchased a few laundry baskets and filled them with sodas, snacks, games, or movie rental coupons as prizes. A local soft drink supplier donated bottled water, ice, and the cooler to hold the water. There was no pressure for students to participate in any events; they were free to grab cookies and a water and leave. The focus was simply to show the library as a welcoming area on campus with the resources to help students academically. Forcing students to take a library tour or participate in the prize drawings would have negated the original goal. The event was deemed a success by faculty and staff, and students appreciated the offer of free water and snacks on a hot day. After the event, thank-you letters were sent to every vendor who donated prizes or materials. A list of donated items was also displayed in the lobby of the library during the event.

With the experience of the first event in 2001, the team found working on the event for 2002 a little easier. One major change was having the event for one day instead of two; the time was also changed from 10 AM to 2 PM. The theme for the second welcome to the library event was "What's in Your Library?" Interior display cases on three of the library floors were again used to display library resources and materials for students to view and answer questions on the prize cards about the displays. This served two purposes: students could view library resources, and they would have to go to the different floors of the library to answer the questions. The planning team hoped the students might find intriguing titles and decide to look around on the various floors. Tours of the library were offered at set times during the event, but they were rarely utilized by the attendees. The free snacks consisted of cold bottled water, chips, and cookies for the students. The brown lunch bags with bookmarks, pencils, and candy were again made available for the students, with seven hundred bags distributed during the event. With the success of the first event, the planning team solicited additional prizes from offices on campus and from businesses in town to supplement the budget. A conscious decision was made to not approach the same businesses every year to ask for donations. Letters were sent thanking the businesses for their donations, and a poster board in the lobby of the library listed the business and the prize they donated. Although faculty and staff were not required to participate in the event, several volunteered to work and hand out the snacks and drinks or collect the prize entry cards. An original goal for the planning team was to create a way for students to learn about the library resources and meet the faculty and staff of the library without the pressures or concerns of looming assignments. The event was again viewed as a success by the faculty, staff, and students.

Publicity was an important aspect of planning for the welcome events. Colorful posters and flyers were distributed across campus and displayed in the library lobby, and sidewalks were chalked with the event information. An article describing the event was placed in the campus newspaper, and a local television station covered the event. Although publicity was very important to the success of the event, the planning committee looked for inexpensive ways to advertise, preferring to spend the allotted funds on prizes and food.

FROM WELCOME TO THE LIBRARY FAIR TO THE EXTRAVAGANZA

The arrival of a new dean of library services in 2003 brought about significant changes to the library fair. The event was renamed the Extravaganza and mandatory attendance was required for all library employees. The event was lengthened one hour to accommodate students with later classes, running from 10 AM to 3 PM, and was dramatically increased in size, from two tables in the lobby to the entire first floor of the library. An Extravaganza Planning Committee was created, with subcommittees for food, decorations, and prizes. Volunteers were solicited to work on the planning and subcommittees.

Planning for the Extravaganza starts several months in advance of the yearly event. The planning committee started meeting in January of 2015 to plan the September event for that year. Monthly meetings occur as the date draws closer, then meetings are increased to twice monthly and then weekly about two months before the event. Every year, an e-mail is sent to all faculty and staff in the library asking for volunteers for the subcommittees.

Floor preparations are underway the day before the extravaganza, a member of the decorating committee starts blowing up Mylar balloons, tables are set up on the first floor, and signs are hung above the tables with the title of the resource displayed on the table. The colorful Mylar balloons are scattered throughout the first floor, adding a festive feel to the event. Furniture is moved around (and to other floors) to accommodate the tables and the large amount of foot traffic during the event.

On the day of the Extravaganza, work starts early to insure everything is ready for the 10 AM opening of the event. Brightly colored tablecloths cover the tables, and staff and faculty bring the laptops from their offices to use at the tables. Balloons, inkpads, stamps, and hand sanitizers are also placed on the tables. The Systems department installs monitors on the tables so visitors can look at the resources being demonstrated electronically. As the opening to the Extravaganza draws closer, the atmosphere in the library becomes charged with excitement and the crowd builds in the lobby. When the Extravaganza is officially opened by the dean of the library, students are greeted by library administrators and handed a plastic gift bag from the library. Among the items in the bag are an attendance card and a small gift from the library. Past gifts have included lanyards, ice scrapers, collapsible water bottle, highlighters, staplers, and portable cups with lids and straws. All of the gifts are library branded. As the ISU and Terre Haute communities roam around the first floor, they are greeted by library faculty and staff eager to show off new services or databases. Seven of the nine librarians in the reference and instruction section choose a database or resource to demonstrate. Resources can be new databases or bibliographic tools, or a service offered to help the university community. A librarian works the reference desk and is usually very busy during the Extravaganza. Another librarian serves as a floater, relieving the librarians at their tables for breaks and lunches. A student worker usually sits at the table with the full-time employee to stamp the attendance card the student presents to each table. The card is very important, because students must visit a set number of tables, listen to the information given, have the card stamped for that table, and turn the card in to be eligible for prizes. Students are encouraged to visit the tables and have their card stamped so they are eligible for a variety of the prizes available. The reference librarians give a two-to-three-minute talk about the resource they have and answer any questions. The reference librarians realize that students may be on a short break between classes or have a limited amount of time to attend the Extravaganza, and it is important for the students to be able to visit several tables to have their card stamped. In 2014, the Prize Committee received 1,078 cards of students hopeful of winning a prize. Students must listen to the talk before their card is stamped. All ISU library employees are encouraged to wear ISU clothing, often a T-shirt designed by the Public Relations department for the event.

In addition to the tables staffed by reference librarians, other departments from the library provide information on interlibrary loan, rare books and special collections, and government publications. Cunningham Memorial Library is a government depository library, and it is important to showcase resources available from the government. Free materials are ordered from the federal and state government, and displayed on a table for participants to take with them. The free items usually include folders, pens or pencils, a state map, and a book with information on events (fairs, craft shows, holiday celebrations) held throughout the state of Indiana.

One particular item was very successful for a few years: the candy jar count. A large clear plastic jar was filled with a variety of candies. Students had to guess the number of pieces of candy in the jar, and the student with the closest winning number won the jar. One year a student guessed the exact number of pieces in the jar. This activity always generated a lot of interest, so someone was stationed by the jar because students often wanted to pick it up or shake the jar. The only rule was that the jar must remain on the table, students were free to walk around the jar or squat down to look at it—but no touching!

The event is so popular that campus organizations have requested to participate in the Extravaganza. Any organization participating must be open to all students on campus. A variety of campus groups have opted to participate in the event, including Student Media, Student Conduct and Integrity, Math and Writing Center, American Democracy Project, Performing Arts Series, Diversity Office, Recycling, University Speaker Series, Center for Research and Creativity, and the Office of the Dean of Students. This is an excellent opportunity for campus groups to showcase their mission and reach a large number of students.

At 3 PM, the event ends and the tear-down begins. Tablecloths are removed and discarded, balloons are collected, deflated, and stored for the next year. The food area is cleaned and pizza boxes disposed of. Refuse is a concern during the event, and trash cans are emptied throughout the day. Signs and furniture are removed within a couple of days, and the library first floor returns to normal.

Prizes are awarded throughout the Extravaganza; winners are notified, and they have a period of time to pick up their prizes. The winners are listed on a poster board in the library.

Publicity was again an important factor in advertising the event. With an increased budget for the extravaganza, bookmarks and banners were created for the event. Bookmarks were handed out at the circulation and reference desks, and large plastic banners were created and placed between concrete pillars on campus. The library homepage advertised the event several days in advance. Brightly colored flyers were distributed across campus, and librarians and staff talked about the event during library orientations and instruction sessions. Every effort was made to insure that the campus community was aware of the event.

FOOD AT THE EXTRAVAGANZA

The Events Area on the first floor is transformed into the food area for the Extravaganza. Mylar balloons shaped like pizza and popcorn decorate the space. Tables and chairs are set up for people to use, although students often eat sitting on the first floor of the library. The food and drinks are available for the five-hour event.

Food is a very important item at this event. After trying other options, the Extravaganza committee determined that pizza was the easiest and most successful choice for food. The Food committee is charged with determining the amount of pizza and drinks needed for the event. In 2014, 550 pizzas were ordered for the event; ISU has increased the student population this year so the library will order more pizzas to accommodate the increased student body. One hundred twenty-five pizzas are delivered hourly until the last hour of the event when the last fifty pizzas are delivered. The pizzas include cheese, pepperoni, and sausage. A bid system determines which pizza business will be used to deliver the pizzas to the library. The bid-winning business also supplies the napkins for the event, with the library supplying the paper plates. The library employees plating the pizza are careful to avoid cross-contaminating the pizza to insure no one violates religious dietary restrictions. Servers plate either the cheese or one of the meat pizzas, but they do not move between the meat and cheese choices. People go through a line to pick up their pizza, but they are asked to only take two slices at a time. They can go through the line as much as they want to pick up additional pizza slices. Indiana State University is a one-soda-company campus. That business provides the library with a variety of sodas and cold bottled water for the event. Sodas are set up on a separate table from the pizza, and students can choose from a variety of regular and diet soft drinks or water. To insure speedy delivery of cold and fresh drinks, paper cups are set up on a table, filled with soft drinks and moved to another table for people to pick up. Again, they can return as much as they like for additional drinks. The Food

Committee plans for five thousand people attending and orders about forty canisters of soft drinks.

Another food option is fresh popcorn, provided by the library's own popcorn machine. The popcorn is freshly popped throughout the day and is located on the opposite side of the floor from the Events Area, giving visitors an opportunity to have a snack as they wander around the first floor of the library. Both pizza and popcorn have proven to be popular items for event.

The Extravaganza has moved from a very small event highlighting library services to a campus-wide event celebrating library and campus resources. In 2001, the first year of the library fair, about 700 students participated in the event. In 2014, the count for the day was 4,309 ISU and community members in the library.

THE EVENTS AREA

The Events Area is a dedicated space for speakers, events, classes, and a Finals Breakfast for students at the end of fall and spring semester. This multipurpose area on the first floor of the library is very popular, and provides a place to host events for the library, campus, and community. The area was created in 2008 and is about six thousand square feet, seating between three hundred fifty and three hundred seventy-five lecture style. Originally, the space was not separated by any sound barriers from the rest of the first floor, often causing noise issues. The situation was rectified in 2009 with the addition of a glass wall separating the area from the rest of the first floor (Hine, 2009). During the summer of 2014, three screens were added to the room; each screen is 69" x 110". One screen is located in the middle of the wall behind the podium and the other two screens are located several feet from the center screen. Television screens are located toward the back of the space on two pillars to increase viewing for those seated in the back of the room. The screens allow all participants in the room to easily view any presentation, from a PowerPoint to a film. A mobile podium with an attached microphone is available or a portable microphone can be used; the options increase the potential for use of the room.

Numerous events have taken place in the space since 2008, and the space has become the location to meet for library events. Campus faculty are honored during the annual Authors and Artists Reception held in February. The reception was started in 1985 as a way to honor faculty who had written or edited a book or created a performance in theatre, music, or another artistic forum during the previous year. During the event, the books are displayed while the librarian who is the liaison for the discipline reads a short biography of the author and asks the author to say a few words about the published work. The faculty member receives a plaque from their discipline librarian.

Faculty enjoy the recognition of their work by the library (Miller, 2015a). The Bakerman Student Research Award is also awarded during the Authors and Artists reception. The Bakerman recognizes excellence in a research paper submitted for a class the previous year and honors students for their skill and originality in incorporating the resources and services of the library. One undergraduate and one graduate winner are selected every year, with the undergraduate winning $1,000 and the graduate winner receiving $1,500. The review panel for Bakerman submissions consists of a librarian and members of the university community (Miller, 2015b).

Additional uses of the Events Area include the two-day Work-Life Conference, where aspects of trying to balance work and life issues are discussed. Guest speakers and ISU faculty address the myriad topics surrounding this issue. Classics Fest is held every semester to celebrate the ancient Roman and Greek civilizations and literature; students prepare posters and presentations for the celebration. Classes often request the use of the room to show films or present speakers; a recent class listened to a crime scene investigator from a local law enforcement agency discuss his job.

Not all events are academic; Indiana State University is working to insure that employees have a healthy lifestyle. Wellness Screenings are an annual event, allowing the employees to obtain vital health information about themselves. Another event that proved very popular was voter registration for an upcoming election. The process was open to everyone in the county, and several university and community members took advantage of the ability to register on campus. The library also supports various causes in the community via fundraisers held in the Events Area. In the past, the library has held two fundraisers every year. Silent auctions and lunch events (baked potato bar, chili) have helped the library raise funds to donate to organizations within the county. Past recipients of the funds raised have included the Court Appointed Special Advocates (CASA), a youth center, and Habitat for Humanity (Miller, 2015c).

The size of the Events Area, plus the ability to serve food (and a small kitchen next to the area) make this a campus and community choice for events. In 2014, 120 events took place in the library and 18,900 people attended the events.

THE EVENTS COORDINATOR

This chapter would be remiss without emphasizing the importance of the events coordinator in managing the Extravaganza and the Events Area. Hired in 2008, the coordinator is responsible for coordinating the Extravaganza and planning the master schedule for that day. Every aspect is detailed, from allotting the various duties and lunch times to assigning trash and cleanup detail. It is important for an event this size to have one person in charge who is cognizant of the many aspects it takes to make the event a success. The coordinator is also in charge of the Events Area, again with many duties for this particular area. The coordinator is responsible for booking the room and confirming reservations, reserving the correct number of chairs and tables for the events, ordering food and drink as requested, and insuring all electronic equipment is functioning for events. Having an event coordinator insures that the many details of the Extravaganza and planned events in the library are met and the occasions are not marred by missed details or a lack of planning.

CONCLUSION

The Extravaganza and the Events Area have given the library a very visible presence on the campus of Indiana State University. Both resources allow the library to showcase the materials and services available to the university and community. The library looks forward to using both items as a way to illustrate the importance of libraries to universities and local communities.

The author would like to thank D.M., M.M., and C.B. for their assistance in providing information for the chapter.

REFERENCES

Hine, B. N. 2008. "Cunningham Memorial Library History, 1870–2008." http://library.indstate.edu/about/units/admin/CML_History.pdf.
———. 2009. *Annual Report Cunningham Memorial Library, Indiana State University 2008/2009.* http://library.indstate.edu/about/units/admin/Annual_Report_2009.pdf.
Miller, M. 2015a. "Library Annual Events: Authors and Artists Recognition Program and Reception." Indiana State University Library. http://libguides.indstate.edu/AuthorsArtists.
———. 2015b. "Library Annual Events: Bakerman Student Research Award." Indiana State University Library. http://libguides.indstate.edu/Bakerman.
———. 2015c. "Library Annual Events: Library Fundraisers." Indiana State University Library. http://libguides.indstate.edu/content.php?pid=325212&sid=2663135.

Chapter Four

Librarians as Event Coordinators

Building Partnerships and Engagement through
User-Centered Programs

Joe C. Clark

The roles of academic librarians have rapidly evolved over the last few decades. As the nature of collections and information access changes, professional duties will continue to develop to meet user needs. A shift from collection-centered to engagement-centered academic libraries, which may create new expectations for programming, is occurring. As Karen Williams noted, academic libraries are moving away from products of scholarship to supporting the process of scholarship (2009, p. 3).

In an effort to facilitate this transition, university libraries have begun to incorporate new and expanded librarian functions into institutional documents. Williams, currently at the University of Arizona, mentions "exhibit and event planning" among librarian roles (2009, p. 5). Other institutions are doing the same; Kent State University's libraries added "exhibit and event planning" to the list of emerging roles and responsibilities of subject librarians (Kent State University, 2014). Some university libraries (including University of Washington, n.d.; University of Pittsburgh, 2012; University Library, University of Illinois, Urbana-Champaign, 2012) articulate duties for subject librarians that do not explicitly include events, but do relate to areas such as outreach, marketing, and engagement. Many of these activities (e.g., promoting the library, creating partnerships, fostering communication, better understanding patron needs, building strong relationships) can be achieved to varying degrees through event programming. As libraries open up areas formerly housing print materials, more space becomes available for other purposes. The transition to digital collections may also alter the way university administrators think about what librarians do. Hence, by providing events that enhance the student experience, their contribution to the institutional mission is more obvious.

Programming in academic libraries is not a new phenomenon; however, the number and variety of events will likely increase. Whether by offering space for the arts (Beahan, Graveline, and Taxman, 2009), taking the lead role in a collaborative film series (Peairs, Urton, and Schenck-Hamlin, 2007), or implementing other creative programs (Karle, 2008), the establishment of a welcoming, user-friendly environment that encourages student participation and learning raises the profile of the library.

This chapter examines two distinct types of library events: outreach and engagement/collaborations. Examples of each come from Kent State University's Performing Arts Library, which hosts over thirty events every academic year, as well as from other University Library departments/branch libraries on the Kent State University campus. The objective is to inspire librarians to consider what types of programs might work in their unique environment and to build on best practices learned at Kent State.

Outreach events are designed to engender awareness of the library and its resources by drawing potential users into the physical space. Engagement programming provides students with real-world experiences that are closely related to their studies. The goal is to support the process of scholarship and experiential learning through value-added activities that contribute to the curriculum. These permit the library to directly impact the student experience, and they usually involve collaborations with constituent departments, schools, and colleges.

OUTREACH

Outreach events inform potential users about library services and spaces. For established patrons, these affairs prompt goodwill and opportunities to interact with staff in an informal setting. Kent State University's Performing Arts Library utilizes several such events, most with specific audiences in mind. Recuring ones include Welcome Week @ the Performing Arts Library, Student Appreciation Day, the Annual Open House, and receptions for the Kent/Blossom Music and Porthouse Academy summer programs.

Welcome Week @ the Performing Arts Library, which has evolved over several years, takes place every semester and targets students who are unfamiliar with the Center for the Performing Arts building (home of the Performing Arts Library). It usually includes four days of activities over the course of one week. Currently Mondays and Tuesdays are "meet and greets," with librarians on hand to visit with students and discuss their studies, as well as introduce library services and spaces. Welcome Week is a good opportunity to let students know how librarians can help them, and for students to put names and faces together.

Activities and themes vary for the remaining days. They have included an ice cream social, gentle yoga sessions, and a day when video and board games are available for students. The game day typically involves an appearance by the University Libraries' black squirrel mascot, juggling lessons, and scavenger hunts with prizes. The latter activity allows librarians to better acquaint users with the library's services and resources. A raffle is also held during Welcome Week. Students can win gift bags containing sundry items with the library logo (e.g., water bottle, tumbler, flash drive, pens, carabiner keychain, USB car charger, and a $20 University Bookstore gift card), all in a reusable cloth bag.

The Annual Open House occurs in the fall, the Student Appreciation Day in the spring. Both follow the "meet-and-greet" format of Welcome Week. The Open House includes performances and comments by deans and directors. Strategically planned one to two weeks before spring midterms, Student Appreciation Day is an opportunity to thank students for their hard work and remind them that the library is there to help them succeed.

Other effective outreach events at Kent State University libraries include Late Night @ the Library, Stress Free Zone, International Student Reception, and Destination Kent State, all of which take place at the main campus library. Late Night @ the Library features food and games on the Friday before the fall semester begins. Aimed at both incoming freshmen and returning students, it occurs from 10 PM to 2 AM, and draws approximately twenty-five hundred students. The main campus library also hosts a Stress-Free Zone, which features popcorn and therapy dogs during finals week. This program was attempted at the Performing Arts Library but was unsuccessful due to the nature of the finals schedule of most of the library's users. Since each library has a unique constituency and needs, librarians should determine what would be most appropriate for their environment.

The International Student Reception, a partnership with the Office of Global Education, is held at the beginning of each semester in the main library. Both the library and the Office of Global Education promote it, and over two hundred come to enjoy food, a short program, and giveaways. Destination Kent State offers tours and overviews of the Main campus library during summer's new student orientation. Light refreshments are provided, and the "Parents Suite" (consisting of bottled water and refreshments) is tremendously popular.

ENGAGEMENT AND COLLABORATIVE PROGRAMS

Engagement events build on existing student programs and interests. They are typically collaborative; librarians work with faculty and/or nonlibrary administrators in planning and/or execution. The Performing Arts Library hosts a number of these, including the Open Mic Lunch, The Director Speaks, the Performing Arts Library Colloquium Series, Performing Arts *Live*, Jazz Café, and career-related programs within the School of Music.

The Open Mic Lunch, while ideal for students in the performing arts, is open to all. Performers have included students from all disciplines, faculty, and members of the community. Although the School of Music has a Student Recital Series throughout the semester at noon on Thursdays, a less formal performance venue (especially for non-music students) did not previously exist. School of Music students are one of the largest built-in constituencies. When planning each event, librarians invite ensembles or studio instructors from the School of Music to participate. This event is now in its fifth year. It averages thirty-eight attendees, and has featured poetry, dance, music, acting, spoken word, beat-boxing, and stand-up comedy.

The Director Speaks began solely as a Performing Arts Library venture, but gradually turned into a true collaboration between the Performing Arts Library and School of Theatre and Dance. It presents director(s), designers, and choreographers (when applicable) discussing their behind-the-scenes creation of a major production. The Director Speaks targets two student populations: theatre majors and minors, and students in the Art of the Theatre class (a general education Kent Core offering). Librarians offer the director a schedule of Art of the Theatre classes, and the event is planned for a time when at least two of the said classes meet. Since instructors usually bring their students, a core audience is guaranteed. The average attendance is eighty-five, and the highest numbers were over one hundred fifty. As a result of its success, The Director Speaks is now held in one of the building's theatres. Librarians received funds to record each event for online viewing.

In spring 2011 the Performing Arts Library Colloquium Series began to provide students with an opportunity to present their research in a conference-like setting. Although participation in the series is open to anyone, topics must be related to performing arts. Attendance is usually low, averaging fifteen; however, faculty and librarians consider it one of the most important library event offerings. Instructors of small graduate seminars have required their students to present, and papers from the series are sometimes accepted for both regional and national conferences.

Based on the success of the Colloquium Series, librarians requested monies to fund the Excellence in Research Awards, which were in place for the 2013–2014 academic year and included a top and honorable mention prize for both graduate and undergraduate papers. Using the university's Digital

Commons platform, librarians founded the online journal *Excellence in Performing Arts Research*. This annual digital publication publishes the award-winning papers.

In addition to disseminating student research, the Performing Arts Library Colloquium Series provides opportunities for panel presentations and lectures by visiting scholars. For example, a panel was put together on Autism and the Arts with a guest professor along with Kent State faculty from various departments.

The Performing Arts *Live* Series is a lecture/recital format. It started in Fall 2013, and to date, all presenters have been faculty or visiting scholars. Librarians target courses that are related to presentation content, the instructors of which typically offer extra credit to their students. The focused promotion and connection to the existing curriculum has resulted in excellent attendance.

A collaboration between the library and jazz faculty, the Jazz Café transforms the Performing Arts Library Reading Room into an intimate club setting featuring Kent State's jazz combos. Students in the jazz program benefit from this performance venue before their semester concert. The Jazz Café usually occurs once a semester, and has created a wonderful rapport with the library and Jazz Studies.

One successful approach to developing collaborative programs is to determine possible voids in the student experience and then suggest partnerships. Performing arts librarians noticed that a number of School of Music students hadn't given much thought to their future, and approached the school's director about collaborating on a careers event. She enthusiastically embraced the idea. They decided on a panel format, as it would allow a number of perspectives on issues to be addressed. The initial program, entitled "Looking to the Future: Careers for Music Majors," prompted the Performing Arts Library to create a special Careers Collection, as well as a paper and electronic guide focusing on aspects of employment in the performing arts. The event was well attended (seventy-five students) and resulted in the program "Stand Out from the Crowd: Applying for Music Positions" two years later, which included members of the Cleveland Orchestra, the superintendent of the local school district, and an individual from the university's Career Services Center. This well-received series continues with new panel programs every year or two, and helps facilitate communication between the library and the School of Music.

When possible, special onetime events (like the career-related programs with the School of Music) are coordinated with existing committees or groups within the collaborative unit. Career events are scheduled during the existing School of Music Convocation Hour, with the assistance from the School of Music committee that oversees it.

DISCUSSION

Selecting library events to stage can be a difficult task. The number of programs is limited by available staff and their existing commitments. Predicting which events will be most impactful is not a science. Kent State librarians identify opportunities that complement constituent populations' activities, or in the case of outreach, may engender a wider awareness of the library and its services. Potential partners have embraced most ideas, and only rejected those with objectives thoroughly met in existing courses (such as career preparation for theatre students).

All of the events described here have specific goals and audiences. After each, library staff met to discuss whether or not it was successful, should be continued/repeated, and if so how it could be improved. Most evolved from modest beginnings and have become part of the institutional culture at the University.

First, the core and secondary audience for each event is determined. Next, a day and time when most can attend is chosen. The Director Speaks events occur when at least two Art of the Theatre classes are meeting. One Performing Arts *Live* event was scheduled as part of a class in a larger lecture hall but opened up to the public, guaranteeing a large audience.

Strong partnerships with departments, programs, and faculty assist in turning out the core audience. This can take the form of a class coming to an event, offering extra credit to students, or promotions and reminders. Such relationships allowed Performing Arts Library staff to conducted twenty-three class "pop-ins" to core curriculum classes during the Spring 2015 semester. These brief (less than four minutes) sessions promoted awareness of library spaces and services, and reached over eleven hundred students.

The Colloquium Series provides a specific example of how working with faculty ensures an audience. Several instructors who teach small graduate seminars (fewer than five students) require their students to present their research. Friends and family frequently attend. At a recent Colloquium featuring an emeritus professor, two instructors offered extra credit to their classes, which helped draw a crowd of ninety-four.

Many of the collaborations described here not only share planning, promoting, and/or execution, but also funding. The Performing Arts Library funding partnerships include the College of the Arts paying for half of the Performing Arts Library Colloquium Series Excellence in Research Awards, and the School of Theatre and Dance contributing to the cost of recording The Director Speaks.

All Performing Arts Library events originally took place in the library's Reading Room, but some now occur elsewhere because they draw more attendees than can be accommodated. Modest renovations in the Reading Room have created a more flexible space.

Most events include light refreshments catered by the University's Banquet Sales unit. This arrangement allows staff to focus on the logistics. Some of the first events, however, involved staff purchasing refreshments off campus (with mixed success). The current arrangement is much more efficient in that it enables one librarian to prepare an event space with student help. Refreshments draw attendees and help to provide an event atmosphere.

Branding is an important element for the ongoing series, most of which have their own logo created by University Communications Office students. Ideally a logo has several iterations: a thumbnail, a vertical and horizontal form, and come in both color and black-and-white. These permit advertising in a number of settings, including online, flyers, quarter-sheet handouts, etc.

Promotion takes a number of forms, including sidewalk chalk, easels signs around the building, social media, listserv messages, flyers in faculty mailboxes, and feature articles in the student newspaper. The reusable easel signs made out of corrugated plastic provide an 8½" x 11" document holder that allows for display of program details. Outreach events that run for a substantial amount of time, such as Welcome Week, involve student employees handing out quarter-sheet flyers at the major entrances to the building housing the Performing Arts Library. The small flyers have event information on the front and an itemized list of services, spaces and hours on the back. Personal invitations are one of the most effective means of promotion. Library staff begin publicizing upcoming events two weeks in advance.

CONCLUSION

While these specific events will not transfer to every library, the concepts behind each do. Determine what programs would be most suitable for your environment and constituents. Academic programs and courses offer built-in audiences. Librarians can discuss possible programs with faculty and administrators, and determine what would best complement the existing student experience.

One of the biggest drawbacks of programming is that it takes time away from other activities. The payoff, however, can be substantial. Students in several 2014 focus groups responded positively to the library's events, indicating that they create a sense of community. Of the Open Mic Lunches, students remarked that they enjoy the opportunity to perform in a less formal atmosphere than a School of Music event, and that the variety of presentations are greatly appreciated. Most of the focus group students signaled that the library events are very important to them. One graduate student who presented research at the Colloquium Series stated that the experience was very important for her professional development. Additional benefits of programming include:

- Creates and strengthens relationships with constituent faculty and departments
- Facilitates rapport with students
- Builds community
- Draws in new users
- Serves as a recruitment tool for the School/College/University
- Connects to institutional goals and mission
- Provides evidence of student engagement opportunities for accreditation purposes
- Offers a value-added feature for students, faculty, and community members
- Presents development officers with an event to bring prospective donors
- Gives the library staff a chance to collaborate, and possibly have fun
- Raises the visibility of the library across campus and community

As you begin programming, be bold and creative and don't worry about failure or perfection. Make changes to subsequent events to improve them. Kent State librarians have used short surveys to determine the demographic information of attendees and to gauge participant sentiment. Most series started slowly, so patience is also required. The first Director Speaks event had about twelve in attendance, and now averages over seventy-five people. Over time event series become part of the institutional fabric, and users know about the events and make inquiries about upcoming programs.

The rapid evolution of academic libraries currently under way is undeniable. The expectation of subject librarians is also changing, and they must keep pace in creative and innovative ways. By programming, librarians can enrich the student experience, build community, and raise the libraries' role in contributing to student success.

REFERENCES

Beahan, Michael J., Laura K. Graveline, and Jennifer R. Taxman. 2009. "Uncommon Partners: Facilitating Creative Collaborations in the Arts Across Campus." *College & Undergraduate Libraries* 16: 194–210.

Kent State University Libraries. "Emerging Roles—Reframing Librarian Roles—LibGuides at Kent State University." Accessed November 24, 2014. http://libguides.library.kent.edu/content.php?pid=474254&sid=3883403.

Karle, Elizabeth M. 2008. "Invigorating the Academic Library Experience." *College and Research Libraries News* 69 (3): 141–44.

Peairs, Rhondalyn, Ellen Urton, and Donna Schenck-Hamlin. 2007. "Movies on the Grass: Encouraging Epiphanies through Experiential Learning at Kansas State University Libraries." *College and Research Library News* (July/August): 444–47.

University Library, University of Illinois, Urbana–Champaign. "Subject Specialist Task Force Report." 2012. Accessed January 16, 2015. http://www.library.illinois.edu/committee/exec/policies/SubjectSpecialistTaskForceReport.html.

University of Pittsburgh Libraries. "External and Internal Communications Research and Educational Support DRAFT." 2012. http://d-scholarship.pitt.edu/15984/10/RES_External_and_Internal_Communications_Plan.pdf.

University of Washington Libraries. "Subject Librarian Position Description Framework—UW Libraries StaffWeb." Accessed January 16, 2015. http://staffweb.lib.washington.edu/units/cms/sl-portal/knowing/position-description-framework.

Williams, Karen. 2009. "A Framework for Articulating New Library Roles." *Research Library Issues* 265 (August): 3–8. http://publications.arl.org/rli265/4.

Chapter Five

Digital Engagement in Delivering Library Services

A Case Study from the State Library of New South Wales

Kathryn Barwick and Mylee Joseph

The State Library of New South Wales is the oldest library in Australia (State Library, New South Wales, n.d.). It serves the people of the state as both a large research library and a memory institution, focusing on the documentary heritage of life in New South Wales, including the European exploration of Australia and the impact of British settlement on the original inhabitants, and providing a range of services and events across the state. New South Wales covers more than three hundred thousand square miles with a population of more than seven million people (NSW, 2014).

The Library uses social media channels to deliver services in four different ways:

1. developing and promoting of library events, exhibitions, products, collections, and services;
2. promoting discovery of library assets, including collections, services, events, exhibitions, online services, physical spaces, and staff expertise;
3. engaging with clients and the community in their preferred channels and online communities; and
4. collecting social media content for the collection, including gathering social metadata contributed by the community.

These activities would be similar in many library environments, including most academic libraries.

ASSETS AND AUDIENCES

In developing strategies for engaging with online communities, library staff identify both assets and desired audiences, a strategy adopted from the Digital Engagement Framework (Visser and Richardson, 2013, pp. 22–28). Library staff choose the social media channels that are both a good fit for reaching the desired audience through online communities as well as those that allow the library to communicate its content, values, and brand effectively. This approach is flexible to cope with the shifting audiences and popularity of different social media tools, as well as scalable for small campaigns to promote library awards and fellowships and for much larger initiatives such as planning the engagement activities for a specialist section of the library's services or a major project such as the World War I anniversary commemorations.

The range of assets includes the library's extensive digital and physical collections as well as the expertise of staff, services onsite and in regional areas, events, exhibitions, online databases and services, the Ask a Librarian service, reading rooms, study spaces, and Wi-Fi. Meanwhile, the library's audiences are wide and varied, encompassing researchers, students, and readers of New South Wales as well as the many people interested in Australia's history and literary heritage. This audience includes many special interest groups, for example cartographic enthusiasts, history teachers, digital scholars, multicultural communities, indigenous communities, and public library colleagues.

SOCIAL MEDIA CHANNELS

The reader may imagine that Australians use the same social media channels as their North American counterparts; however, there are some differences in the popularity of tools across the various communities around the world. In choosing a social media tool in which to invest staff time and share library content, the potential Australian audience (Cowling, 2014) is considered as well as international audience trends. The terms of service that apply to a social media channel, together with considerations of copyright, accessibility, and privacy obligations as well as the online community's own etiquette also guide selection.

In choosing social media channels to suit library purposes, the ability to include live links back to library domains and corporate branding that is consistent with the library's online presence is also considered. In most cases, banners or icons are created specifically to fit the tool, and a cautious approach to moderation and interaction is also explored in order to maximize engagement while minimizing risks to the brand and reputation. Benchmarks from other galleries, libraries, archives, and museums (GLAM organizations) are also identified, with many examples inspiring library activities. Where an idea like "Made with the British Library" on Pinterest works particularly well, the State Library has sought permission from the other organizations to imitate the initiative.

STAFF SKILLS

During an intensive two-year project (2012–2014), working groups of library staff successfully piloted a range of social media tools through a four-stage process; assessing, exploring, engaging, and evaluating each tool and its effectiveness to deliver library services (Joseph, 2013). The four stages were designed to be a transferrable skill set, applicable to any new social media tool that staff may encounter, and guiding staff in decision making when an exit strategy from a tool is warranted. Table 5.1 lists the four-stage process and the knowledge and skill sets for each.

Table 5.1. Transferrable knowledge and skills for digital engagement

Stage	Knowledge	Skills
Assessing	• terms of service • content ownership • copyright • privacy • accessibility • records management • are there alternative tools? • popularity of tool	• locating terms of service, copyright, accessibility, and privacy information for a tool • applying library policies to determine suitability of tool • determine target audiences • writing a brief for approval to initiate an official account
Exploring	• community guidelines • features of tool • types of content that can be shared • importance of mobile options	• establishing account(s) • establishing workflows • creating content • navigating approval processes for use of library content • applying copyright law and Creative Commons licences • capturing business records • collecting social metadata • documenting procedures • installing and testing app versions
Engaging	• meaning of community member interactions • library incident procedures • comfort with change in the interface or app versions	• finding relevant content / accounts and interacting • interacting with other community members • building following / audience • testing all different features of the tool • cross-promoting via other tools and the library websites • answering enquiries • adapting to change in the social media tool • understanding the community "ownership" of all shared content, especially where it can be curated and further shared (e.g., reblogged, retweeted, repinned)
Evaluating	• tracking statistics in the tool (e.g., followers, notes, likes, reblogs, views, use) • tracking incoming hits to library domains from social media tools	• interpreting social media tool statistics • setting up and interpreting Google analytics • accounting for staff time • analyzing audience development, message amplification, reach and impressions data

Prior to these working groups, the use of official social media tools to represent the library had been limited to a few authorized staff with a primary focus on marketing library activities. The working groups had a much wider brief to engage with the communities online and explore the potential for service delivery in these channels. The number of social media tools emerging, the volume of content required to keep channels active and current, and the need to monitor and respond to community interactions presents resourcing challenges. A more distributed staffing model was sought, drawing on staff from a wide range of roles and specialty areas across the library and facilitated by online engagement training for all the staff involved in working groups. Staff create social media content in their areas of expertise and are encouraged to be creative, providing varied perspectives on the range of activities at the library (Reddacliff, et al., 2013).

The six working groups of library staff volunteered to pilot five social media tools, including two of the groups working on contributing relevant content to Wikipedia as GLAMwiki editors (Phillips and McDevitt-Parks, 2012) as well as official accounts being established on Tumblr, Instagram, Pinterest, and Historypin. Eight individual social media accounts were established, with all transitioning to business-as-usual following their evaluations. Internal consultation with content experts and experts in services and business requirements (e.g., records management and media communications) ensured that working group members had appropriate guidance in creating content and engaging with online communities.

ENGAGEMENT OUTCOMES

Successful digital engagement for the library takes many forms on social media including:

- geotagged and hashtagged photographs of library buildings taken by members of the Instagram community
- community contributions further enhancing Wikipedia articles created by library staff
- reuse of library images contributed to Wikimedia Commons in articles on the many different language editions of Wikipedia and in a variety of other forums
- reference enquiries via comments on Instagram posts
- reblogging and interaction on library Tumblr posts
- use of Historypin tours on smart boards in classrooms
- individuals curating library content on Pinterest
- comments and interactions on the library's images in Flickr Commons, including invitations for images to join groups

- individuals following the links from social media channels through to library catalogs and websites for further exploration

DIGITAL ENGAGEMENT IN DIGITAL COLLECTING ACTIVITIES

The role of social media in contemporary life poses a digital collecting challenge for libraries, particularly memory institutions like the State Library where collecting the documentary heritage of life in New South Wales includes content shared on social media (Barwick, Joseph, Paris, and Wan, 2013). Social media conversations give an insight into the opinions, concerns, and perspectives of the millions of Australians using these platforms. Understanding how the community engages on social media, the types of conversations that occur, and the role of hashtags and abbreviations become very important in identifying potential content to be collected.

Familiarity with the terms of service, privacy policies, copyright constraints, and legal deposit legislation that applies in social media spaces and different geographic regions is also important in mapping digital collecting workflows. The library used a social media monitoring tool developed by the Commonwealth Scientific and Industrial Research Organisation (CSIRO) to pilot collecting social media content from platforms (Barwick, Joseph, Paris, and Wan, 2013).

Social metadata, the high-value contributions from members of the community that enhance the library's knowledge of a collection item or event (Smith-Yoshimura, 2012), is also a high priority for the library. Locating it, verifying the information, and incorporating it into library records and systems present many challenges for the future.

CONCLUSION

Digital engagement is a continuum; the tools continue to evolve, the formats change and follow fashions and trends in popularity, and the communities shift and migrate to new platforms in ways that require library staff to adapt with them. It seems likely that collection development, long regarded as a core library activity, will increasingly become a more collaborative function with crowdsourcing, community sourcing, community curation, and participatory interpretation influencing the shape of future collections and requiring library staff to be effective at engaging in the digital realms for digital collecting and delivering library services.

REFERENCES

Barwick, Kathryn, Mylee Joseph, Cecile Paris, and Stephen Wan. 2014. "Hunters and Collectors: Seeking Social Media Content for Cultural Heritage Collections." In *Proceedings of the VALA 17th Biennial Conference, Melbourne, 3–6 February 2014*. VALA. Accessed July 17, 2014. http://www.vala.org.au/vala2014-proceedings/vala2014-session-7-barwick.

Cowling, David. 2014. "Social Media Statistics Australia—June 2014." *Social Media News Blog Australia*, July 1. Accessed July 17, 2014. http://www.socialmedianews.com.au/social-media-statistics-australia-june-2014/.

Joseph, Mylee. 2013. "Catalysts, Innovation and Online Engagement @SLNSW." In *Proceedings of the Library and Information Association New Zealand Aotearoa Conference, Hamilton, October 20–23*. http://www.sl.nsw.gov.au/about/publications/docs/JosephMylee-LIANZA2013.pdf

NSW Government. 2014. "About New South Wales." *NSW Government*. Accessed July 8, 2014. https://www.nsw.gov.au/about-new-south-wales.

Phillips, Lori Byrd, and Dominic McDevitt-Parks. 2012. "Historians in Wikipedia: Building an Open, Collaborative History." *Perspectives on History* 50 (9): 55. Accessed July 17, 2014. http://www.historians.org/publications-and-directories/perspectives-on-history/december-2012/the-future-of-the-discipline/historians-in-wikipedia-building-an-open-collaborative-history.

Reddacliff, Anne, Vanessa Tracey, and Kathryn Barwick. 2013. "Pin-Pointing Communities: The NSW State Library's Innovation Project." *Incite* 34 (3): 22. Accessed July 17, 2014. https://www.alia.org.au/sites/default/files/publishing/INCITE_web34.3.pdf.

Smith-Yoshimura, Karen. 2012. "Social Metadata for Libraries, Archives, and Museums: Executive Summary." *OCLC Research*. Accessed July 17, 2014. http://www.oclc.org/research/publications/library/2012/2012-02.pdf.

State Library, New South Wales. n.d. "History of the Library." Accessed July 17, 2014. http://www.sl.nsw.gov.au/about/history/index.html.

Visser, Jasper, and Jim Richardson. 2013. "Part D: Assets and Audiences." *Digital Engagement in Culture, Heritage and the Arts*. Inspired by Coffee. Accessed July 17, 2014. http://digitalengagementframework.com/.

Chapter Six

From Idea to Instagram

How an Academic Library Marketing Committee Created a Character for the YouTube Generation

Joyce Garczynski, Laksamee Putnam, and
Lisa Woznicki

Librarians spend inordinate amounts of time creating help guides and pathfinders, as well as other tools, to entice students to use their services. As more of these items find their way to library websites, course management programs, and other venues, one challenge seems to always rear its ugly head: How does one get students to access and view these tools and take advantage of library services? At Towson University's Albert S. Cook Library, this was a puzzle that many of the librarians tried to solve. Print as well as video tutorials and help guides were created, and flyers and signs were posted around the physical library alerting students to services and policy changes, but these seemed to have little impact (to view the library's current print help guides and video tutorials see http://libraries.towson.edu/help-guides). It was apparent that the library needed to find a new way to reach its students regarding information beneficial to their academic careers as well as to get them to utilize library services. After much discussion, the library's Marketing Committee suggested that a handful of library staffers try their hand at creating an informative but humorous library-related public service video. While none of the staff had any formal experience in film, the group decided to try scripting. They created a quick video that could be used on the library's web page to advertise a change in printing procedure—and the library's Video Subcommittee (and ultimately their YouTube Channel) was born.

The subjects of the initial videos were dictated by the need to inform students of policy and procedural changes at the library. The early video topics included procedures for printing in the library, upcoming programs that the library was hosting for National Library Week, publicizing the library's Amazon.com wish list, and utilizing the library's new text messaging service. In each instance, two library staff members put together a scenario and one created a script. To infuse the project with humor, the original videos were often parodies of popular commercials; the video advertising the new print debit card system was based on the "What Would You Do for a Klondike Bar" commercial showing students going to exaggerated lengths to obtain the new print card. Library staff and student workers were recruited to act in the videos, and props were simple and homemade.

Finding student actors was often a problem, as many of the employees were not comfortable appearing on film. Repeated requests went out to students asking them to volunteer for a few minutes of filming. Usually, the library staff had to approach students individually and plead with them to participate, promising that they would ultimately enjoy the experience. One librarian contacted the Theatre Arts department and tried to find student actors, but because of the students' commitments to departmental productions, they had no time for extra acting jobs and the request met with little success. Because of the small number of available students used as actors, scene changes and transitions were limited. As a result, the Video Subcommittee decided to try using a puppet as a common actor who could be filmed doing an activity while a narration was read over the film sequence. Initially, a ventriloquist puppet was used as a character appearing in numerous videos (see figure 6.1). The subcommittee felt that his attempts to perform activities typically done by students such as typing, dialing a phone, using the library catalog (all filmed showing the puppet's small plastic hands) were very humorous. The videos were all filmed in various locations in the library and were completed without any budget. Upon completion, the videos were uploaded to YouTube and advertised on the library's website. Judging by the comments posted, viewers enjoyed the videos and found humor in the obvious low-budget, homespun quality that was evident in each film. This gave the subcommittee courage to expand their fledgling efforts and attempt longer, more elaborate films. Over time, however, it became apparent that students were identifying the ventriloquist puppet with a horror movie character, and this negative connotation convinced the subcommittee to stop using the puppet, but video projects continued.

UPPING THE ANTE

A more complicated video was planned involving a common complaint in the library about students being too noisy, messy, and generally disrespectful of the space and the patrons around them. The subcommittee designed a video that was modeled after a Liberty Mutual television commercial focusing on the benefits of random acts of kindness. When the Association of College and Research Libraries (ACRL) announced their President's Program Innovation contest (Free, 2011) in early 2011, the subcommittee submitted the Liberty Mutual parody idea and won the "In-progress" category! This positive support provided a higher level of motivation and expectation for the end result. The award enabled the library to recruit and pay student actors. In order to insure student participation, the library advertised for student actors and compensated them for their time with a small cash payment and a pizza lunch. After actors were recruited, students signed recording releases, and filming was completed over a four-hour period. (The completed video, "Civility: That's Our Policy," can be viewed here: http://youtu.be/XHd2tCWFXoA). The simplicity of the video message has allowed it to be shared over an extended period of time, and it is continually aired throughout the year on the library lobby video monitors. Encouraged by the award recognition, the subcommittee envisioned a further series of videos to be produced. The previous award money had been spent, however, and there was still the problem of enlisting student actors.

Figure 6.1.   Image of First Library Puppet. *Image taken by authors*

RETHINKING PUPPETS

Because of the success of the initial videos, the subcommittee began to think about using a different type of puppet, which would eliminate the need to find at least one student actor. Instead, a library employee would take on the role of puppeteer. The previous ventriloquist-style puppet, while fine for the initial "amateur" videos, did not fit with the subcommittee's vision for a higher-quality series. Initially, the new puppet search centered on locating a suitable tiger puppet, a nod to the school's mascot. Finding the right puppet, however, proved to be more problematic than expected. First, if the puppet was to actually speak directly to the camera, a moveable mouth was required. Second, if the puppet was to hold something, or type, it needed to have arms and fingers that could be manipulated by the puppeteer. The subcommittee could not find a tiger puppet that satisfied these requirements. Additionally, the library might have faced problems creating a mascot that did not align with the university brand requirements. One evening, as a committee member was watching a TV show featuring Jim Henson's Muppets, the answer was clear: use a Muppet. A Muppet-style puppet could easily match the mouth and hands requirements, portray a student character in any persona needed for the film series, and lend a sense of whimsy and fun to the message. After a lengthy Internet search, the committee decided to order a blue, furry puppet from the Luna's Puppets website (https://www.lunaspuppets. com/).

BUILDING A CHARACTER

The next step was creating an identifiable character who would be the protagonist throughout the subsequent films. As the puppet traveled on his journey to become "information literate" with the help of the library, the subcommittee hoped students would be able to identify with his experiences. The puppet would be an "information novice" and needed to be paired with an older, wiser student who could show him the ropes. This description became the driving force in creating the initial dynamic between the two main characters; a young, novice researcher with a more experienced guide to lead the way. In searching for a name for the furry character, many possibilities were bandied about, but the subcommittee struggled to find a name clear of connotations of television, movie, and literary characters. Because the library is named for its benefactor, Albert S. Cook, the puppet became Al Burt. Limitations from University Marketing would not allow Al to be called a mascot, so instead his title became "Cook Library's Biggest Fan."

After choosing a puppet, and while developing main characters, a puppeteer needed to be found among the library staff. As a puppet, Al is very easy to control, requiring only one person to move his head and a single arm to animate his hand. A hand could be placed into Al's head either from directly behind through an opening or from his bottom half (the puppet does not have legs). Both his arms are open from the elbow to his four fingers, making it simple for the puppeteer to use either arm (see figure 6.2); however, after a librarian volunteered to act as puppeteer it became clear that practice was required. A master's student in the Theater Arts department who focused his thesis on puppetry provided a basic instruction session. The most important element in puppetry is motion. Even when standing still, the puppet needed to always interact with his environment. As each video was developed and filmed, the puppet became easier to animate, as the librarian became familiar with controlling Al. Specific skills that required practice included connecting voice to mouth movement and understanding the puppet's physical location; because the puppeteer was not able to see through Al's eyes and was often reading a script, it was difficult to make Al speak with emphasis and look at an item or person. Ultimately, practice along with the ability to film a scene and allow the puppeteer to review immediately after filming helped all those involved to improve acting and animation skills. A library film star was born, but he needed a partner in crime.

The subcommittee decided that Al's wiser guide would be his roommate. This would require a single student actor to film a few episodes over the course of the school year. Rather than try to recruit multiple student actors, the subcommittee hoped a single actor would be easier to cast and schedule. Luckily, a theatre student and son of a library employee was willing to sign up and add the film series to his CV. The character he would portray was named "Bill" and the two interacted as if they were both two young students; no references were ever made regarding Al's puppet nature. The relationship between the two was based on the characters Wally and Beaver from the old television series, *Leave It to Beaver.* This meant that in most of the videos, Al gets in trouble because he does not understand how to perform basic research tasks, or avail himself of services offered at the library. This would be followed up with Bill patiently explaining tools like an APA citation guide and services such as Text a Librarian, which allowed Al to complete assignments and survive his first semester at college. The hope was that the video series would appeal to undergraduates: presenting Al as a character unfamiliar with college and learning about all the different ways the library was available to help (see Figure 6.3).

SCRIPTING AND SERIES CONSISTENCY

When the subcommittee began to talk about creating a series of videos featuring Al and Bill, the general consensus was that there would be a series of

Figure 6.2.   Photo of Al and Puppeteer. *Image taken by Kanji Takeno, Towson University director of photographic services*

four initial films focusing on the services that the library wanted to highlight for that school year: outreach research assistance held in academic buildings outside the library, the text-a-librarian service, library help guides for citing sources (specifically APA), and in-person assistance offered at the Research Help Desk. The subcommittee decided to organize the sequence of videos based on their sense of when students might need to use each resource or service. The videos were not meant to be step-by-step tutorials; instead, they served much like public service announcements, pointing students in the direction of resources they could utilize. The subcommittee envisioned each topic as a separate video, much like the episodes in a situation comedy.

Figure 6.3.   Photo of Al and Bill. *Image taken by author*

Therefore, each was given a title and a storyline was created so that viewers would learn about the service but also get to know the two main characters. The initial idea of calling the sequence *The Al and Bill Show* was dropped; instead, the videos were each identified by their title; however, a persistent tagline emerged in every video: "Cook Library Has the Answers" and became the unofficial title of the series. There was a point toward the end of each video where the all-knowing experienced student, Bill, would utter these words or a phrase with the same intent. That phrase was then used as the unifying agent to tie the videos together and help viewers link the library to these services and the characters.

After the primary topic for each show was chosen, a script was written. One key object needed by the puppeteer was a script. The scripts, written by the Performing Arts librarian, set up the scenario, listed props needed, provided actors with overall tone, and gave the videographer directions on focus and transitions. The lines for each actor were never memorized; actors were given the flexibility to change lines so long as the important points were not left out. The script also noted scene locations and a list of props needed for each scene. These choices were influenced by multiple factors. Prior to filming, the videographer and author of the script would block out each scene, visiting the locations selected and taking photos to document the space, placement of windows, amount of light, and any other details that could affect filming. The lighting, available outlets, homemade props, and pieces of furniture all needed to be considered and, if possible, written into the script to help everyone understand how filming would progress. Overall, the script helped build consistency throughout the video series, by describing each individual storyline and ensuring that it connected to previous videos.

Additionally, "Cook Library Has the Answers" included a variety of features that linked videos and made them identifiable as a series. For example, each video began with the same music. The soundtrack was selected from Soundtrack Pro, a royalty-free music application offered by Apple. The opening sequence always introduced the two main characters, Al and Bill, and provided the episode title, similar to modern television shows. After the opening sequence, the episode would begin by clearly identifying campus buildings where the primary scenes were taking place. Each video lasted between two to three minutes in duration, based on the subcommittee's understanding that students would not want to watch anything much longer (Attebury, 2010).

Initially, the videos included cutaway scenes that added content that was strictly for entertainment purposes—a practical joke played by Al, or a silly stunt that was referenced in conversation between Al and Bill; however, these sequences added to the length of the scripts and made filming complicated. After the subcommittee held focus groups asking students for their critiques of the series, it was decided the cutaways diluted the informative message of the videos. The next "season" in the series eliminated the cutaway scenes. The following titles were produced during that initial season of video filming: "Al Finds Research Relief," "Al Discovers Text and Chat," "Who Is Apa," and "Monster Mash Up" (viewable via http://bit.ly/alburtvideos).

CHOOSING LOCATIONS

After the scripts were developed for each topic and settings around campus were selected, filming began! People were alerted if they were included in the background of a shoot but if possible, an early film time or summer time frame was chosen to minimize disruptions. Students seemed to enjoy seeing Al being filmed, however, which often led to students snapping a photo and being directed to the library's YouTube channel to find out more.

In most cases, the crew was small and consisted of the puppeteer; student actor; videographer; and an additional staff person who handled props, microphone, lights, and other technical equipment. Since most of the filming was done on campus, it was easy to load equipment onto carts or, when necessary, into a car to drive to another building. Having compact equipment that can be easily transported and stored in ready-to-go packaging simplified the process. Because the locations had already been examined for lighting and electrical needs and the action sequences blocked, once the crew arrived on the scene, filming could start with a minimum of setup time. In some cases, permission needed to be sought from building managers before the crew could begin setting up equipment, but this was not an issue if filming was done outside of buildings or within the library. The subcommittee tried to make the most of the available space in the library, often using staff areas when filming scenes that were to represent a dorm room or personal living space.

In some cases, a green screen was used if the videographer wanted to edit in background film to complete a scene. Because the library had no budget for this project, the subcommittee used an actual green table cloth, pinned behind the actors. Later, the videographer would edit a different background behind the characters to achieve the desired effect. Props were simple and homemade with household items repurposed for many shots. Al's wardrobe came from a local thrift store, and over the span of a few months, the subcommittee had amassed a number of interesting T-shirts for him to wear. For legal reasons, the crew asked that student actors not wear outfits with designer logos or recognizable images that were protected by copyright. If possible, university-themed apparel was used to identify Al with his school.

When locations were scouted, it was essential to remember that any scene was limited by the physical needs of the puppeteer and the puppet. Because Al does not have a lower torso, he must always be filmed sitting at a desk, table, or behind a counter. Each scene must be carefully staged so that the puppeteer is hidden. In many scenes, a tablecloth was used to cover the open space under a table where the puppeteer was kneeling. The puppeteer often wore a black top that could fade into the background of different camera angles. The crew went to great lengths to make sure that her arms, head, and even her hair were never included within any shot.

The placement of the puppeteer often meant that a microphone needed to be used to make sure that her voice sounded natural on film. In scenes with Al's roommate, the actor could direct his lines across the table to Al, but when replying, the puppeteer was actually below the table's surface and had to work to project her voice. The crew often had to move the microphone in various test positions so that the puppeteer's voice would sound natural on camera, free from echoes, with a sound quality that matched the surroundings.

The puppeteer's work was more physically demanding than the subcommittee had expected. In many cases, she was kneeling for large blocks of time, or sitting on a small step stool. The puppet is covered with faux fur, so it is heavy and holds heat, and to keep him at eye level with his human counterpart, the puppeteer had to keep her arm extended for the duration of each shot. As a result, it was important to build in breaks in the shooting schedule to keep the puppeteer feeling refreshed and energized.

FILM EQUIPMENT AND VIDEO EDITING

The equipment used to film and edit the series has expanded and improved over time. With a limited budget and fast production time frame, however, most of the videos created did not require a high level of technical skill. The videographer involved in creating this series did have a learning curve; his skills in this area were entirely self-taught and when necessary, the University's Electronic Media and Film Department was consulted. Typically, the videographer spent three to six hours per video in post-production editing. Specific hardware and software used for this project will be detailed here, but technology today has made it possible to do most of this from a smartphone alone.

The filming was done on a Canon XHA1 HD video camera attached to a tripod. This camera is tape-based; however, in order to make editing easier a Direct-to-Edit (DTE) recorder was utilized. This digital recorder made it much easier to transfer video to the computer, rather than adding an additional step converting from a tape recording. The camera was usually utilized in an automatic setting; however, this meant that light was an important consideration, and often scenes needed to be adjusted so background windows would not wash out the actors. To fix some of the light problems, a basic soft-box light was used to add illumination without glare. As mentioned previously, a microphone was used to insure the puppeteer could be heard despite needing to be hidden from view. Specifically a lavalier microphone was used by the puppeteer and occasionally a unidirectional condenser microphone was held overhead to capture overall sound. A microphone helps cut back on ambient background noise; however, when using separate microphones instead of the built-in camera microphone, one must be sure everything is connected correctly! A few times, filming needed to be redone because the crew managed to turn the camera on but not the microphones. It is a good idea to record multiple shots of a scene to insure there is enough content to create the video. Additionally, playing back any recordings during the filming process allows everyone to be sure the equipment is working properly and make adjustments as needed. A piece of helpful but not essential equipment is a video monitor, which allows the crew and actors to view how the scene looks from the camera. This is especially helpful to the puppeteer to provide a better understanding of where the puppet appears within the camera frame and how to move in a realistic way.

Filming was done in a 4:3 aspect ratio, to make it easier for the video to be broadcast on various lobby televisions in the library; however, with video quality improvements, a 16:9 ratio and higher definition are preferred. Higher definition is a simple way to make videos look higher quality. Professional quality can also be achieved by editing the video into a cohesive final product. The video editing software used for this series was Final Cut Pro 7;

however, basic video editing can be accomplished through free programs that come with any nonlinear editing software, such as Windows Movie Maker or iMovie. As mentioned previously, adding an opening and closing sequence and soundtrack to the series help tie the videos together. This consistent branding is connected to numerous other projects that involved Al, all of them showcasing a positive message about the library (see figure 6.4).

PROMOTION AND ASSESSMENT

Since October 2012, the Video Subcommittee has released six completed videos starring Al. In order for these videos to effectively promote the library's most underutilized services, they needed to be seen by a wide variety of students. As a result, the library Marketing Committee initially decided to designate the broad category of undergraduate students as the target market for the Al videos.

Since all of the Al videos are listed on the library's YouTube channel (http://bit.ly/alburtvideos) a new video is simple to share. Once a new video is published, the library publicizes the new title by sharing a link to the playlist, which starts with the new content. This approach encourages viewers of one video to check out previous titles that they may not have seen. The link to the new video is then distributed via the library's social media channels (Facebook and Twitter), a spotlight on the library website, and a post on the daily e-mail announcement that is sent to all university affiliates.

The Video Subcommittee thought that undergraduate students who have some connection with the library would be a good market segment to approach, so they devised a series of promotional tactics in an effort to reach that audience. When the first Al videos were released, the Video Subcommittee encouraged all of the librarians who taught library instruction sessions to show these new videos as the students were coming into the room. This strategy takes advantage of the eager-to-learn captive audience that is waiting for instruction to begin. Similarly, the subcommittee created Post-it notes with Al's picture, the words "Have you met Al?" and a link to the library's YouTube channel. These notes were placed at the library's Research Help desk, and whenever a student asked for a book in the library, the library staff members working at the desk were encouraged to write the call numbers down on these branded notes. On more than one occasion, a library patron who received a note asked to know more about Al. In addition, the subcommittee began to use Al to promote other library programs. For example, Al's photo was placed on an American Library Association (ALA) READ poster that hangs on the library's main floor (see figure 6.5), his videos are shown on a loop on a video screen in the library lobby, and the subcommittee created short videos with Al to introduce two contests that the library held to

Figure 6.4. AI in public service poster. *Image taken by Paul Peeling, Albert S. Cook Library technology manager; poster designed by Tiffany Henley*

promote their new Instagram account (http://instagram.com/ cooklibraryoftowsonu/). These strategies are meant to help solidify the connection in students' minds between the library and Al.

About one year after the release of the first videos, the subcommittee decided to expand promotional efforts to attempt to reach undergraduate students outside the library. They decided to hold a launch party for a new Al video in the student union around lunchtime. As students came into the

Figure 6.5.   Al READ Poster. *Image taken by Kanji Takeno, Towson University director of photographic services; poster designed by Towson University Photographic services*

building, they were given candy that included a tag with Al's picture, an encouragement to watch the video, and a link to the library's YouTube channel. Al himself was on hand at the party to sign autographs and say hello. Much to the surprise of the subcommittee, this event did not provide the promotional opportunity that the group wanted. Many students were not interested in the candy or in Al, and said that they did not have the time to take a few seconds to speak to library staff members about the videos. In retrospect, the subcommittee realized that this approach might not have been effective, because students are accustomed to vendors and other organizations using that same space and employing similar tactics to try and sell them things. In addition, some of the students who did stop by said they were not interested in learning more about the videos because Al was "creepy." Given that the launch party strategy prompted less than enthusiastic responses to Al, the subcommittee felt they needed to gather more information about how students perceive Al, the Al videos, and what students think are the best ways to promote both.

In order to gain some clarity about student perceptions of Al and the Al videos, the subcommittee would need to hold focus groups. This research methodology is a fantastic way to introduce new media productions and gather information by informal conversation. Focus groups, however, do not provide data that is representative of the opinions of a whole population, so it is a good idea to hold more than one group on a topic and look for similarities across groups.

The subcommittee held two focus groups related to Al and the Al videos, with a member leading the facilitation. They held the focus groups at lunch-time and offered free pizza as an incentive to participate, but the number of students who signed up for the groups was low until one of the subcommittee members convinced a faculty member teaching a social science research methods class to offer focus group participation as extra credit. Ultimately, the first focus group had three participants and the second had twelve.

In terms of the focus group questions, the facilitator distributed a questionnaire before the group began in order to obtain participants' demographic information such as class and college affiliation. In order to break the ice and get the group participants talking, she began the focus group with the broad question, "What library service do you use most frequently and what is your opinion of that service?" Then the facilitator showed three of the previous Al videos, making sure to show examples that demonstrated both the short, commercial format and others with the longer cutaway segments. Finally, the facilitator asked the focus group participants questions about Al as a character ("If you had to describe Al in one word, what word would that be and why?"), the format and content of the videos ("Which library service or services would you recommend and why?"), and the target market for these videos ("Would you be interested in seeing Al in future library promotions? If so, what should Al promote and why? If no, who would you rather see in library promotions?").

The focus groups yielded information that supported the previous efforts of the subcommittee, and some suggested a course correction might be needed. No one in the focus groups had seen or heard of Al, nor did they think that he was creepy or too juvenile for a college audience, thus the character of Al could remain intact. Many of the focus group participants did take issue with the format and the content of the videos, and these responses suggested a few changes should be made. Both focus groups preferred the shorter commercials to the longer videos with cutaways. Also, participants in both groups said they wanted the videos to be more informative and less focused on entertainment, which they perceived to be a waste of their valuable time. Finally, the groups suggested that the Al videos would best be suited for new or first-year students, because the groups felt that upper-level students should already know about the services promoted.

CHANGES AND LOOKING TOWARD THE FUTURE

Given the focus group feedback that students do not connect Al with the library and that first-year students would most benefit from the Al videos, the new target market for the Al videos has become new students. Al is now a more visible part of the library's program during new student orientation, and a campus-wide program designed to make first-year students feel more comfortable as they make the transition to college. During this orientation, new students who come to the library are given a postcard that has Al's picture on the front, and on the back it lists the top ten things that every new student should know about the library. In addition, students who come to the library during orientation have the opportunity to have their picture taken with Al in a makeshift photo booth. The library then shares these photos on their social media accounts (see photos at http://instagram.com/cooklibraryoftowsonu/).

The content of new Al videos also has changed to reflect the feedback from the focus groups and this new target market. New videos are shorter and no longer have cutaways. Also, the topics covered focus on services that are most beneficial to new students. For example, the first video produced after the focus groups was "Why Cook Library Rocks" (http://youtu.be/FX2pnRxcAg4), which is only a minute and a half long and briefly highlights some of the library's most popular services.

Although the focus groups indicated that students were happy with Al's persona, this new shortened format and new target market meant that the Al character needed a personality change. There was no longer enough time in the videos to establish and build the relationship between Al and Bill. It was necessary for Al to stand on his own. As a result, the character of Bill has graduated, and Al serves as a guide for new students introducing them to library services. The first scene in the "Why Cook Library Rocks" video reflects the attempt to make that transition.

In the future, the Video Subcommittee would like to more firmly establish the association between Al and the library in the minds of undergraduate students. The hope is that by focusing on creating and marketing content that is meaningful to new students, this connection will only grow stronger as each new class enters. In addition, the subcommittee hopes to expand the promotion of the videos on social media. They have established a Facebook page for Al (https://www.facebook.com/cooklibrarybiggestfan), but staff cutbacks and lack of time have prevented this promotional channel from reaching its full potential. By having Al regularly comment on library and campus happenings through social media, he could become part of the campus community and his relationship to the library will only grow.

CONCLUSION

A series of library promotional videos starring a puppet named Al started out as simply an idea. Through careful planning, scripting, and filming, the library struck out on a new path to connect with students. Utilizing popular modes of interaction (social media and YouTube), libraries can move from traditional print communication into an appealing and meaningful conversation with patrons. The key is to remain flexible and listen to users and their habits. Libraries open to popular trends and focused on designing library services centered on the needs of their audience can establish new relationships and deliver service that is more personal. By doing exactly this, the Albert S. Cook Library was able to transform a puppet into an effective promotional tool.

REFERENCES

Attebury, R. I. 2010. "Perceptions of a Profession: Librarians and Stereotypes in Online Videos." *Library Philosophy and Practice* 433.http://digitalcommons.unl.edu/libphilprac/.
Free, D. 2011. "2011 ACRL President's Program Innovation Contest Winners." *ACRL Insider*, June 2. http://www.acrl.ala.org/acrlinsider/archives/3676.

Chapter Seven

Promoting Digital Library Services through Workshops

Tracy C. Bergstrom and Alexander Papson

With the opening of the Center for Digital Scholarship (CDS) within the University of Notre Dame Libraries in the fall of 2013, the university library began offering workshops on a wide range of topics including metadata creation and interoperability, geographic information systems (GIS), text mining, data management, and data analysis. These workshops focus on engaging with students and faculty at the start of their research to inform them of the availability of tools and resources provided by the libraries. The workshops also serve to promote in-library expertise and reinforce the role of the library's institutional repository in capturing research output. The chapter discusses the CDS's successes with workshops as a marketing and outreach strategy to promote digital library services and to attract attention and clientele to the library.

BACKGROUND

The Center for Digital Scholarship in Hesburgh Library, constructed in the summer of 2013 with funding from the University President, advances the vision of the University of Notre Dame to redefine and transform library services and spaces for the twenty-first century. With the CDS, the libraries established a new campus destination where scholars from the arts and humanities, social sciences, sciences, and engineering can work collaboratively on projects using shared technologies and applications. Located in the heart of the main campus library, the CDS incorporates new state-of-the-art technology, high-end software and research data sets for analysis and visualization, and discipline-specific consulting and support. The space supports GIS, data analysis, text mining, digitization, metadata services, and data management planning, all formerly unavailable to the broad campus community.

The newly launched CDS is part of the Hesburgh Libraries' overall strategic initiative to expand digital programs and services in support of the university-wide goal to engage in external collaborations that extend and deepen Notre Dame's impact. This alignment of the libraries' strategic initiatives with Notre Dame's objective to increase its profile as a research institution have promoted the CDS to an endowment priority in the university's current comprehensive campaign. The results of this campaign are intended to continually support growth and technology enhancements. Notre Dame librarians are also actively applying for grants and other external funds to increase the capacity of the CDS. The CDS will benefit, for instance, from having two Council on Library Information and Resources (CLIR) postdoctoral fellows become part of its staff in the fall of 2015.

The staff of the CDS is composed of a program director for digital initiatives and scholarship who leads the initiative, a digital initiatives librarian, a metadata and digital projects librarian, a CLIR postdoctoral fellow focused on GIS and data management, and a digital scholarship coordinator. The libraries' digital projects staff, including a visual resources curator and two media digitization specialists, also fall within the CDS on the libraries' organizational chart. Of these positions, only the digital scholarship coordinator role was created specifically to support the initiative; the position includes responsibilities for scheduling and promotion of the space and services as well as keeping metrics on workshops and other activities. All other positions were pulled from various units within the libraries into the CDS as it was formed.

All librarians within the CDS staff are expected to teach workshops and engage with patrons on behalf of individual research projects. Select colleagues from other departments in the library and graduate students with specialized skill sets also were invited to teach within the CDS. At the start of the academic year, CDS librarians decided that each workshop should include the same baseline information: to provide an overview of all of the center's activities to help clientele become acquainted with the new space and services, to define and provide examples for the current session topic, and to identify CDS contacts for all content areas in addition to that of the session topic. Additionally, CDS librarians identified four tenets to guide those who were creating workshop content:

- Workshops should focus on student and faculty engagement at the start of their research processes to help researchers see the potential value of digital scholarship.

- Workshops should inform participants of the availability of tools and resources provided by the library to reinforce evolving collections and services.
- Workshops should promote in-library expertise, including the availability of librarians and specialized staff within the CDS and subject specialists.
- Workshops should reinforce the role of the university's institutional repository in capturing research output to raise awareness of this resource.

This chapter discusses the lessons learned from this first year of operation, with special emphasis on parlaying workshop attendees into clientele and advocates for the library.

LITERATURE REVIEW

There is no dearth of literature on the topic of conducting successful library workshops that are meaningful to patrons. Veldorf's (2006) ALA guide codifies best practices for teaching hour-long workshops in library settings. Fabian et al. (2003) focus specifically on reaching diverse audiences in academic and special libraries through workshops and other events, including exhibits and kiosks as a means of marketing collections and electronic services. They cite Arant and Clark (1999), who articulate the importance of librarians' abilities to teach about technology and information as distinct within an academic community, although not always recognized by patrons. Silver (2014) states the importance of subject specialists working in conjunction with technology librarians to offer workshops targeted to individual disciplines to meet the wide range of specialized interest and needs found within an academic environment.

Recent literature has also addressed targeting workshops to specific subsets of the university community. Virtue and Esparza (2013) document their efforts to keep faculty abreast of digital trends, both to increase their knowledge of emerging technologies and to raise faculty awareness of library instructional programs. The successes of workshop series for graduate students are recorded by Alvarez et al. (2014), who noted that graduate students wished for more discipline-specific as opposed to interdisciplinary content, as well as a conversational tone within workshops to encourage dialogue. Mularski and Bradigan (1988) also recommend that support staff within a university such as administrative and research assistants are excellent targets for library workshops, as they are prime utilizers of the library and have influence on the work of others in a variety of roles around them.

Literature about teaching the concepts supported by Notre Dame's CDS varies by topic. Sweetkind-Singer and Williams (2001) initially raised the necessity of supporting a new technology service, in their instance GIS, through outreach via workshops targeted to individual departments. More recently, Houser (2006) documents that GIS outreach and its resulting connections with researchers are vital to building a sustainable service that responds to user needs. Mayer and Goldenstein (2009) note the importance of workshops when dealing with visual materials that are of increasing importance to a variety of disciplines, yet are less well understood than textual library resources. Johnson and Jeffryes (2014) suggest teaching concepts as multifaceted as data management through multipart, flipped workshops series. Through this literature review, the authors were unable to find any information about other libraries offering metadata workshops, so this may be a topic currently emerging in library instruction.

RESULTS

Over the course of the 2013–2014 academic year, the CDS librarians and affiliates offered forty-seven workshops, not including special events such as faculty discussions and instruction sessions limited to particular classes or groups. These workshops were open for registration to anyone with a campus NetID. In total these forty-seven workshops attracted 246 attendees, who represented a mix of affiliations and departments from across the university. Class sizes ranged from twenty participants, the maximum capacity of the center's classroom, to a single, devoted student. Workshop topics varied from introductions to a particular subject, to specialized classes such as Using Python in ArcGIS and Analyzing Articles Using JSTOR's Data for Research Service. Overall, the breakdown of workshops offered was as follows: fifteen sessions about GIS, thirteen about text mining and analysis, nine about data use and analysis, six about metadata and data management, three about digital scholarship in general, and one about 3D printing. Attendance patterns generally followed the overall availability of workshops, with GIS workshops attracting the most participants over the course of the academic year.

At the end of the academic year, the digital scholarship coordinator analyzed the overall inquiries received by the CDS in person, via e-mail, and by phone. These ranged from general questions such as "How can I arrange a tour for my students?" to requests for highly specialized project support. These inquiries mirrored the workshop offerings in a relatively similar fashion: the most frequently utilized service area was GIS (31 percent), followed by text mining and analysis (24 percent). General questions such as inquiries about space utilization or hours of availability comprised 11 percent of inquiries. Specialty printing and scanning, including inquiries about the 3D printer, large-format and high-resolution scanners (11 percent), and data use and analysis (10 percent) were the next most frequently utilized service ar-

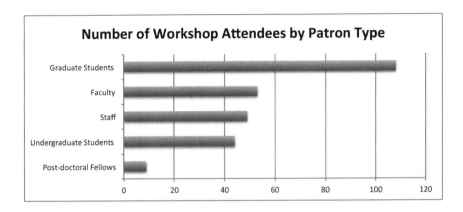

Figure 7.1. *Created by author*

eas. Requests for digitization (7 percent) and for assistance with metadata and data management (6 percent) rounded out the topical inquiries.

The correlation between workshop offerings and inquiry topics confirmed what the libraries had learned when conducting an environmental scan while planning for a then-forthcoming CDS in the spring of 2013. In this scan, in which the digital initiatives librarian spent 20 percent of his time over the course of three months interviewing faculty and staff from across the university to assess unmet needs, GIS, data, and text analysis were identified as most conspicuously lacking broad support on campus. This combined data also provided the support to increase the CDS's staff. During the first year of service, GIS-related offerings were taught by a CLIR postdoctoral fellow initially funded for only two years. By having the metrics to demonstrate the high level of interest in this service, the program director successfully lobbied to make this position permanent.

Discrepancies between the workshops and inquiries illuminated areas in which the CDS needed to bolster workshop offerings and recruit campus colleagues or graduate students to teach. It was not surprising, for instance, that there was such an interest in the libraries' new 3D printer, but none of the CDS librarians possessed the appropriate knowledge to teach a variety of sessions on its potential usage. The CDS's one workshop offered on 3D printing in the first year was taught in the spring semester by a master of fine arts in industrial design graduate student with experience in makerspace environments, and was quickly filled with a wait list. Topics under the rubric of data use and analysis also received interest from individuals in a variety of disciplines that utilized statistical tools, so Notre Dame's economics librarian teamed up with some of the university's statistical consultants to offer specialty workshops on R, Stata, and other specialized software.

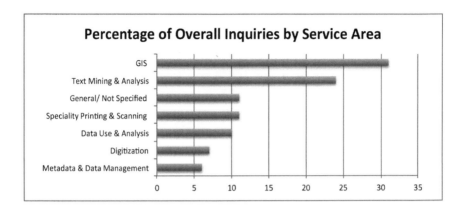

Figure 7.2. *Created by author*

Of no great surprise was the discrepancy between the relatively low number of faculty who attended workshops and the high number of faculty inquiries into the CDS's services. Faculty asked 39 percent of overall inquiries
across topics within the first year of operation, but accounted for only 20
percent (53 of 263) of workshop participants. For faculty that did attend
workshops, the library saw benefits as described by Virtue and Esparza
(2013): faculty gained awareness of digital scholarship tools, but perhaps
more importantly became knowledgeable of the libraries' new roster of service offerings and spoke about them with colleagues and students. Several
particularly fruitful collaborations within the first year resulted in publications and presentations that were coauthored by faculty and CDS librarians
who had contributed to project methodologies and outcomes. As one of the
initial goals within the CDS was to reposition its librarians as research partners rather than assistants, this became a way in which success could be
measured within the center.

Graduate students, on the other hand, accounted for 41 percent (108 of
263) of workshop participants, and asked 25 percent of overall inquiries
across topics within the first year. Particularly evident was graduate students'
willingness to engage with CDS librarians to formulate workshop topics that
would be of practical interest and to discuss their research methodologies and
tools. A group of political science graduate students, for instance, requested
that a targeted workshop be offered to address GIS techniques applicable to
their research. All CDS librarians now also spend considerable amounts of
time discussing individual research projects with graduate students on a one-
on-one basis. This has several direct benefits: CDS librarians are mindful of
trending student and faculty research areas that might be better served in the
future through expanded services or workshops; librarians become ac-

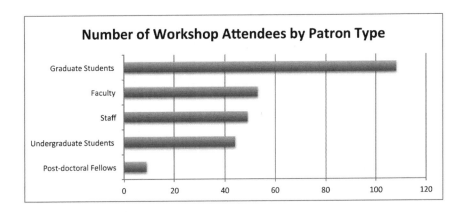

Figure 7.3. *Created by author*

quainted with the students, who are then targeted for hire as evening and weekend staff; and the libraries benefit heavily from word-of-mouth promotion among students and their peers.

Several workshops had faculty and graduate student participants that attended with the specific intent of learning new skills to start a research project. After better understanding the potential complexities of a topic through a workshop, for example metadata preparation, these individuals consulted with CDS librarians to guide them through various phases of their projects. This enabled CDS librarians to involve other individuals in the library system, often including subject specialists, and raise patron awareness of the variety of expertise available through the library. These projects also helped develop partnerships with other groups on campus, including departments and other research centers, and allowed the library to become a destination for interacting with a wide range of research tools and new technologies. As a result, this has opened doors for other collaborations and helped develop new ideas for future projects with current partners.

The CDS also saw a noteworthy number of university staff as workshop participants within the first year, accounting for 19 percent (49 of 263) of overall workshop attendees. Several productive collaborations resulted between the libraries and other administrative units on campus as a result of some of these attendees. A CDS librarian, for instance, advised on the digitization of historical issues of the *American Catholic Studies Newsletter*, published by Notre Dame's Cushwa Center for the Study of American Catholicism. Contacts made through workshop attendance also helped create new connections for CDS librarians with other technology and support staff around campus, including within professional graduate programs, specialty or discipline-specific centers on campus, and the Office of Informational Technologies.

Undergraduates attended various workshops, but in slightly lower numbers than other groups. As CDS librarians had initially perceived that the primary clientele for instruction was faculty and graduate students, the majority of workshops were offered during the day or early evening at times convenient to these groups, but perhaps less so to undergraduate students with a full roster of classes and other obligations. Undergraduate students tended to interact less in workshops and not to contact the CDS with follow-up questions in significant numbers. CDS librarians have worked with several undergraduates working on research projects or theses that heavily utilized the center's services; some of them initially came to the library through workshop attendance and some were referred by their faculty advisors. CDS librarians have also interacted with a few undergraduate students that attended workshops and then returned the following year as graduate students, and subsequently approached the CDS with specific questions to develop a new project or to further advance their skills.

While CDS librarians were pleased overall with workshop attendance and resulting interactions within the first year, registration statistics at the end of the year indicated an initial saturation of the market. While GIS and text mining classes had often averaged seven or eight students in the first semester in the fall of 2013, a year later they were averaging three or four students per session, with several sessions cancelled because of zero registrants. The program director and digital scholarship coordinator perceived this as a need to change the outreach and engagement strategy, and reach out to disciplines and programs with which the CDS had previously had few interactions. CDS librarians also began offering multipart workshops and pursuing the option of graduate students receiving official recognition of attendance on their curricula vitae with the Graduate School.

It was also apparent during the CDS's initial year that its services were being evaluated by various groups on campus to see the potential for various departments or disciplines to adopt the technology. For instance, the School of Architecture experimented heavily with the CDS's 3D printer and then subsequently purchased its own. As a result, CDS librarians realize that they will need to stay relevant by looking to new technologies and continually evolving the center's workshop offerings. As CDS librarians continue to consult with various groups, they also learn of unmet needs that may be beneficial to develop as future areas of instruction; in Notre Dame's case, video production and editing are skills in need of generalized support on campus. These needs propel librarians to broaden their own areas of in-house knowledge as well as continue to forge connections with others on campus that might offer workshops in the center's environment.

CONCLUSIONS

The variety of faculty, staff, and student attendees to workshops within the CDS's first year of operation gave great insight into future directions that would be appropriate for the Center to pursue. While some of the CDS librarians' initial presumptions about desired services were confirmed through attendance and inquiry numbers, in other instances they were made aware of areas in which there was great interest, but for which they would need to expand the service and teaching roster to accommodate the need. This gives the libraries solid data for funding applications and internal position requests in regard to desired future areas of growth. Of great importance were also the personal connections forged between CDS librarians teaching workshops and individual attendees seeking specific areas of assistance. Faculty and graduate student attendees in particular became the CDS's best public relations tool, as they spread word-of-mouth recommendations to colleagues for workshops and consulting services. Resulting collaborations, including numerous coauthored papers and presentations, also bolstered the CDS's credibility within the university community.

REFERENCES

Alvarez, Barbara, Jennifer L. Bonnet, and Meredith Kahn. 2014. "Publish Not Perish: Supporting Graduate Students as Aspiring Authors." *Journal of Librarianship and Scholarly Communication* 2 (3): 1–10.

Arant, Wendi, and Charlene K. Clark. 1999. "Academic Library Public Relations: An Evangelical Approach." *Library Administration and Management* 13 (2): 90–95.

Fabian, Carole Ann, Charles D'aniello, Cynthia Tysick, and Michael Morin. 2003. "Multiple Models for Library Outreach Initiatives." *Reference Librarian* 82: 39–55.

Houser, Rhonda. 2006. "Building a Library GIS Service from the Ground Up." *Library Trends* 55 (2): 315–26.

Johnson, Lisa, and Jon Jeffryes. 2014. "Steal This Idea: A Library Instructors' Guide to Educating Students in Data Management Skills." *College & Research Libraries News* 75 (8): 431–34.

Mayer, Jennifer, and Cheryl Goldenstein. 2009. "Academic Libraries Supporting Visual Culture: A Survey of Image Access and Use." *Art Documentation: Journal of the Art Libraries Society of North America* 28 (1): 16–28.

Mularski, Carol A., and Pamela S. Bradigan. 1988. "Library Workshops for Special Audiences: Secretaries, Research Assistants, and Other Support Staff." *Bulletin of the Medical Library Association* 76 (2): 151–54.

Silver, Isabel D. 2014. "Outreach Activities for Librarian Liaisons." *Reference and User Services Quarterly* 54 (2): 8–14.

Sweetkind-Singer, Julie, and Meredith Williams. 2001. "Supporting the Information Needs of Geographic Information Systems (GIS) Users in an Academic Library." *Information and the Professional Scientist and Engineer* 16: 175–91.

Veldorf, Jerilyn. 2006. *Creating the One-Shot Library Workshop: A Step-by-Step Guide*. Chicago, ALA.

Virtue, Alicia, and Loretta Esparza. 2013. "Faculty Reconnect: Creative Outreach to Keep Faculty Up-to-Date in the Digital Whirlwind." *College & Research Libraries News* 74 (2): 80–99.

Chapter Eight

It's the End of the World as We Know It . . . or Is It?

Looking beyond the New Librarianship Paradigm

Rebecca Parker and Dana McKay

Librarianship is often described half-jokingly as "the second oldest profession" (Myburgh and Tammaro, 2013). Not wishing to take the analogy too far, it could be said that the two oldest professions share their basis in a service culture, where the customer is always right and every need is catered to. But for libraries at least, this hasn't always been the case.

Part of the charm of libraries and the appeal of the profession is that libraries provide their services free of charge. Rather than being perceived as devaluing librarians' skills by giving them away, libraries are seen as having more intrinsic worth because of it. Yet in an increasingly competitive higher education environment, academic librarians are a conspicuous target. Libraries cost money, and they don't (obviously) make any. Higher education is rapidly changing, and for the first time libraries and librarians are challenged to justify their value as well as their cost.

This book series looks at librarianship in the twenty-first century, where the role of the academic librarian has expanded to include research metrics, open access, data curation, repositories, and many other areas conceived of as "a new librarianship." In addition to these new concepts, librarians still retain their traditional skills of information organization, collection management, and reference. This blend of old and new has made libraries indispensable to their parent universities in the first decades of the century. But how long will this last? Like any forward-thinking profession, it is time academic librarians looked into the crystal ball and made some predictions for the future. Are library skills still valuable? Are librarians ready to embrace the *next* librarianship?

This chapter looks at how academic librarians' skills can be applied to areas outside libraries, where they are much in demand. These include corporate information management, knowledge management, intranets, search engine optimization, business analysis, enterprise architecture, information policy, and learning space management.

THE REPORTS OF MY DEATH HAVE BEEN GREATLY EXAGGERATED

There have been many gloomy prophecies of the death of libraries. The first came with the burning of the Library of Alexandria, where humanity lost great works by ancient dramatists, poets, philosophers, and scientists. It was impossible to think that the world could ever recover from such a tragedy. And yet, while that event—and any book burning that followed it—is synonymous with the repression of knowledge and loss of culture, the human race did recover. We do once again hold works in our libraries that show the earth orbits the sun.

Messages of doom for libraries have reappeared at regular intervals over the centuries, usually accompanying any major new development in technology: from the printing press to the paperback to the e-book. The common denominator for all of these revolutionary inventions is that they allowed greater availability of information, whereas once libraries had been the gatekeepers to all the knowledge of the world. They threatened (or at least were perceived to threaten) libraries' way of life, their very existence. Gutenberg's press printed books in the language of the commoners. Development of the paperback brought affordable books into the homes of ordinary people. Providing texts in e-book format allowed more than one library user to have access to the same book at the same time. And web search engines let users develop their own queries, without the need for the complex syntax that drove early online databases and required a skilled professional to navigate. Google has been around since 1999, and electronic texts longer than that. We are another generation further on from this, and guess what? Libraries are still here.

Anyone would think librarians are simply afraid of change. And yet rather than putting them out of a job, technology has become a great enabler for librarians. They are frequently early adopters of scientific advancements (such as the Internet and 3D printing), and they seek ways to bring these resources to others in an affordable and equitable way. This increasing availability of information over time, rather than depreciating the value of the profession, has reinforced the need for someone to organize and classify knowledge so others can navigate the morass. It seems laughable now that librarians would ever have opposed the idea of openness to information when it is now so integral to the practice of modern librarianship. And yet in some ways they did.

The State Library of Victoria in Melbourne, Australia, opened in 1856. It is a remarkable building, funded by the Victorian Gold Rush of the 1850s, and designed to rival the splendor of other cities around the world (particularly Sydney, Melbourne's arch-rival to the north). The library was a symbol of the growing colony's aspirations to be a "free and secular society where knowledge was made visible and accessible" (Edquist, 2013) and books were stored on open shelves to enable library visitors to help themselves. At the heart of the State Library is the magnificent Domed Reading Room, opened later in 1913. Modeled on the British Museum and the Library of Congress (Edquist, 2013), the room is octagonal, and at its heart features a raised dais where the librarian once sat, looking down on library users and maintaining order.

For modern librarians, this layout is immediately jarring. It is difficult to believe that as little as a century ago, library spaces were still designed to put librarians at a distance from library users, and in such a clear position of authority. On entering an academic library now, visitors are likely to see

Figure 8.1.   The Domed Reading Room in the State Library of Victoria. *Image copyright 2014 Dana McKay*

spaces founded on principles of flexibility, openness, and learner-centered design (Brodie, 2008). It couldn't be further from the architecture of the Domed Reading Room.

And it is not just library buildings that have changed. As universities evolve, the role of the academic librarian shifts from information broker to trusted partner in teaching and research. Librarians have increased the scope of their work to show value to their parent organizations in ways unimaginable twenty years ago: If librarians hadn't adapted, academic librarianship would have gone the way of the dinosaurs long ago. Yet there is no doubt that academic libraries are challenged as well as driven by these sweeping changes and subject to shifts in the mood of the higher education landscape. Public libraries, while pushed to cut costs, are rarely questioned on their value, as they serve an acknowledged dual role as a community hub. Academic libraries do not have the same protection: Their users may conflate libraries very closely with the physical buildings, not realizing that the library is also providing access to the information they are consuming by the gigabyte (Tenopir et al., 2009). When this happens, and administrators hear "We don't use the library," academic libraries are at risk (Hinze et al., 2012). So how should academic libraries demonstrate their value?

THE ORIGIN OF THE SPECIES

One of the first lessons for any student of librarianship even now is Ranganathan's five laws of library science (Ranganathan, 1931), which espouse that:

1. Books are for use.
2. Every reader his [or her] book.
3. Every book its reader.
4. Save the time of the reader.
5. The library is a growing organism.

All librarians, regardless of field or generation, tend to agree that these laws are the basis of the philosophy on which our profession is founded. Yet for many modern librarians, the five laws are beginning to look quite dated. They don't support growing diversity in technological means of accessing information, and are fixated on a single information medium—one that is itself used less and less, particularly in academia (Talja and Maula, 2003). Crawford and Gorman (1995) breathed new life into the manifesto and brought it to a new generation with their 1995 revision:

1. Libraries serve humanity.
2. Respect all forms by which knowledge is communicated.

3. Use technology intelligently to enhance service.
4. Protect free access to knowledge.
5. Honor the past and create the future. (p. 8)

This framework is better suited to the new librarianship paradigm than Ranganathan's original, especially for academic librarians. It will be used in this chapter to explore how roles outside the library using existing skills can still be a good fit for librarians' professional principles and practice.

FOR WHOM THE BELL TOLLS

So far, the changes to libraries described in this chapter have failed to toll the death knell for the profession. Yet change is definitely on the horizon. Vendors are providing many outsourced services that libraries used to perform themselves, including affordable digitization, shelf-ready print collections, and patron-driven acquisition. Book cataloging roles are morphing into repository metadata expertise, discovery layers, and search engine optimization. Libraries have moved from buying all their content through subscriptions to publishing some open access content in-house.

Librarians have transformed with modest success from the print environment to online, but librarianship as a profession needs to prepare for what will come next. When asked in 2013 what the future of libraries would look like, Samantha Schmehl Hines of the University of Montana suggested that "Maybe . . . the librarian becomes the library" (Hines, 2013). In accepting this view, libraries shift the focus from the functions of the library to the skills and characteristics of the librarian. In Australia, most library schools have converted the course to a postgraduate qualification. In the United States, the head of the academic library is a dean. Worldwide, there is heated debate within the profession (and there has been for some time) about whether librarians should have PhDs. In the new librarianship, research skills can be seen as a bonus in dealing with complex data curation issues and tricky research questions. Focus for a moment, though, on a different upside to this apparent inflation in qualifications: Even librarians new to the profession bring with them a wealth of skills, knowledge, and training from other domains that serves to enrich, diversify, and invigorate the profession. Hahn (2009) notes that:

> [Librarians] cannot be expert themselves in each new capability, but knowing when to call in a colleague, or how to describe appropriate expert capabilities to faculty, will be key to the new liaison role. Just as researchers are often working in teams to leverage compatible expertise, liaison librarians will need to be team builders among library experts where this advances client research. (Hahn, 2009, p. 2)

With the variety of skills librarians now bring to the profession, they cover more bases than ever before. It would be a valuable undertaking to research which fields new candidates come from, to identify the gaps, and to look at where it might be beneficial to recruit the next generation of multidisciplinary librarians. Clark (2014) encourages librarians to explore how "their own more esoteric skills may be useful in the library setting" (p. 11). Will this lead to mission creep? Almost certainly. So what? As the former university librarian at Swinburne noted almost five years ago (Whitehead, 2010), the profession is rapidly moving away from the "cosy library" (the home of traditional library roles, collections, and spaces) toward the "scary library," where the role of the librarian is less and less familiar. Librarians need to embrace change as a constant in the profession. The academic librarianship community needs to work out how to handle the heat, or get out of the kitchen.

IN A PARALLEL UNIVERSE

A recent tweet from @LousyLibrarian (2015) detailing a conversation with a library user indicates that librarians are not alone in prophesying their own doom:

> @LousyLibrarian: "Hasn't the internet basically made the library obsolete?"
> "The internet has also made saying dumb opinions out loud obsolete."

Are librarians an endangered species? Is it time to give up, or to fight back? Crawford and Gorman's revised five laws of library science (1995, p. 8) are excellent weapons against claims that librarianship is an artifact of the past. These principles provide a clear framework for applying traditional librarianship skills to a new information age. Looking through the lens of these five new laws, a number of career areas outside libraries where library skills are in considerable demand become apparent. These opportunities can help librarians advance their own goals, while at the same time assisting in the achievements of parent organizations.

Critical thinking and active listening are capabilities identified as important for librarians, and also transferable across and between professions (Clark, 2014, pp. 12–13). One field that requires these skills and uses them in a similar way is business analysis. This discipline is defined as "the set of tasks and techniques used to work as a liaison among stakeholders . . . to understand the structure, policies, and operations of an organization, and to recommend solutions that enable the organization to achieve its goals" (International Institute of Business Analysis, 2009). Business analysis is often aligned with the IT function in an organization, but it has a lot more to do with information flow than it does with engineering solutions.

Requirements elicitation, a key activity of business analysis, is the process of working with stakeholders "to identify and understand their needs and concerns, and . . . the environment in which they work" (International Institute of Business Analysis, 2009). Business analysis is often linked to systems and solutions, but it need not be—successful business analysts often don't have a technical background, but must be able to understand how an organization functions, including its goals, processes, and intended outcomes. This is where critical thinking and good communication skills—key skills of the librarian (Clark, 2014)—come to the fore. In his definitive text on reference work, Katz (2002) identifies that above all, the capable reference librarian must have "an ability to talk to all types of people, to find out what they need" (p. 13). Business analysts similarly provide a bridge between business users and the system implementation team.

The parallels between business analysis and the reference interview are apparent. Methods used to elicit requirements in business analysis take many forms, including workshops, structured interviews, business process mapping, and the application of standard techniques for prioritizing requirements. The task for business analysts during requirements gathering is to "ensure that a stakeholder's actual underlying needs are understood, rather than their stated or superficial desires" (International Institute of Business Analysis, 2009). This echoes the words of Katz (2002) when he notes that "librarians tend to ask enough questions to clarify the real needs of the user rather than accept what may be only a weak signal for help" (p. 16). Ethnographic studies of reference librarians show that what they do in practice is very like what Katz teaches (Crabtree et al., 1997; Nordlie, 1999).

The requirements-gathering function can be a challenging activity for business analysts and reference librarians alike. Business analysts will often identify contradictory requirements from different areas of a single organization. Business analysts, like reference librarians (and, hopefully, lawyers), try to avoid leading their subjects toward a preferred conclusion or putting words in their mouths. Communicating requirements back to the organization, resolving conflicts, and identifying priority requirements are critical skills of the business analyst. This is not so different from the reference librarian, who requires the "ability to take a jumbled query, sort it out, reword it, and feed it back to the person who put the question as if it was his or hers" (Katz, 2002, pp. 24–25).

As described above, the business analyst's role and ability is to work with business stakeholders to identify requirements and needs. This is a role compatible with the traditional skills of the librarian, and it may not require indepth technical knowledge for librarians to transition to these roles—though it may require additional skills and qualifications.

Many academic librarians, however, are more interested in and proficient in the technical aspects of information work. Since the early days of computers, these librarians have tended to gravitate toward roles such as the systems librarian. Within the modern university, however, there are other information technology fields that go deeper into the functionality of and relationship between organizational systems. These new roles have connections for, and may suit, some technically minded library and information professionals in the future.

One example is enterprise architecture. This field emerged in the 1980s as a means of addressing significant organizational IT problems: the rising cost and complexity of systems, and the poor alignment of these systems with organizational needs (Sessions, 2007). The role is seen as "appl[ying] archi-tecture principles and practices to guide organizations through the business, information, process, and technology changes necessary to execute their strategies" (Federation of Enterprise Architecture Professional Organiza-tions, 2013, p. 1). The enterprise architect role is perceived as having a "unique blend of skills . . . including business, information, and technology competencies" (Federation of Enterprise Architecture Professional Organiza-tions, 2013, p. 8).

Is this blend really completely unique? Once again, comparisons with the modern multidisciplinary librarian should be drawn. Enterprise architects work with experts from a range of "inter-connected disciplines"—including risk management, information management, and metadata management—as well as with technical disciplines (Federation of Enterprise Architecture Pro-fessional Organizations, 2013, p. 7). These domains are areas of expertise for librarians, especially those with a background in corporate information man-agement.

The enterprise architect requires a number of skills common to the tradi-tional role of the systems librarian, such as systems analysis, data structures, database design, and vendor management (Wilson, 1998, pp. 65–66). An awareness of the strengths and weaknesses of open source software is essen-tial to the modern enterprise system landscape. Libraries actually have a head start here—they have supported the open source software movement for some decades through digital libraries (Greenstone); repositories (DSpace, Eprints, and Fedora, to name a few); discovery layers (VuFind); and integrat-ed library management systems (Koha and Evergreen).

In addition to systems librarianship, it is also possible to draw a compari-son between enterprise architecture and information organization. Both re-quire an understanding of types and structures of information. Being able to recognize how information (and data) flows through an organization is essen-tial to effective management of its enterprise architecture.

Librarians have been applying authority control on author names since 1647, when the Bodleian librarian grew frustrated with the numerous spellings of Shakespeare's name, and filed them all under a single entry in his library's catalog (Weinberger, 2007, p. 67). Name authorities are just one form of controlled vocabulary that exists in libraries. As librarians have understood for a long time, common terminology enables more effective retrieval. Since the advent of user interfaces, implementing controlled vocabularies in dropdown menus has also made it easier for users to choose from or enter a set of predetermined metadata elements. For creators, this decreases the effort required to add descriptive elements to new information (Foster and Gibbons, 2005; Koppi, Bogle, and Lavitt, 2004), an activity which in turn aids searchers in their quest for information.

Enterprise architecture has a companion concept in the common information model. These models enable data exchange between distributed systems (Quirolgico et al., 2004) and simplify integration between applications—in essence, to ensure that when enterprise systems talk to one another, they use the same term and have a common interpretation of its meaning. This benefits the organization by making it easier and cheaper to add or remove individual systems (Fulton, 2005, p. 78) from the enterprise architecture (think Lego) without dismantling the whole stack (think Jenga). It seems likely that the need for these models will become even more pressing as enterprise systems move to the cloud and are no longer hosted, managed, and controlled onsite.

The need for and value of common information models is recognized by technologists, but the creation and maintenance of these ontologies is a role they may look to libraries to perform. One of the authors of this chapter has developed such a model to aid enterprise architecture practice at Swinburne. Any librarians with a background in metadata and taxonomies, an understanding of systems, and familiarity with the organizations in which they work, are equal to the task.

Librarians of the future should be looking for roles that bring together all their strengths and areas of expertise, as repository work did in the 2000s (Parker, 2008). The technology strategies of universities reveal a focus on ensuring return on IT investment, including the issues surrounding the move to cloud-hosting of enterprise systems. The shift to cloud infrastructure for large technology-hungry organizations like universities requires skilled contract negotiators. It also requires information professionals with a sound understanding of data retention and intellectual property issues. Librarians who have been working in repositories and other digital libraries could be well placed to step into these roles.

LET'S GET PHYSICAL

So far this chapter has focused on where academic librarians might be able to find new roles that make use of their existing skills and expertise. But what about traditional roles that can be expanded to meet the needs of a future generation of library users? While it is certainly true that requirements for in-person reference services and book loans have diminished over the past few years (Martell, 2007), library physical spaces are still very much in use (Bailin, 2011). Libraries are one of the places American parents look at (Foster and Gibbons, 2007) when helping their children to select a college (thereby also selecting where they are investing large sums of money). The library where the authors of this chapter work is frequently over capacity (McKay and Buchanan, 2014).

What, then, is going on out there in the buildings—and what does it have to do with modern librarians? The issue of library design is seen more and more in the literature—what users want and how to create it. Perhaps the most important work on academic libraries is that of Foster and Gibbons (2007). They used an ethnomethodological approach to determining what students wanted in an academic library, and how the library fits into students' days. They found that the library existed as a sort of "third place": somewhere to go between class and home, and that students used it for eating, sleeping, solo study, and group work. These same activities are seen in other studies, both in the United Kingdom (Bryant, Matthews, and Walton, 2009) and Australia (Bailin, 2011; McKay and Buchanan, 2014)—group work and solo work, and social time as well.

When academics talk about physical libraries, if they work in institutions where there is sufficient library space for them to use the library without disruption, they often wax lyrical about a quiet place to read, and (like students) speak about libraries as a "third place" (Stelmaszewska and Bland-ford, 2004; Buchanan et al., 2005; Makri et al., 2007; Tenopir et al., 2009). The academic perception of libraries is much more in keeping with the hal-lowed halls of academia that nostalgic traditionalists yearn for (Mann, 2008). There is certainly a place for this, but library buildings are also being put to different uses. With an increase in the number of group assignments (Cain, 2013), academic libraries have become a hub and meeting space for this work to take place (Foster and Gibbons, 2007; Bryant, Matthews, and Wal-ton, 2009; Bailin, 2011; McKay and Buchanan, 2014).

Things have changed: It is a rare day that the reference desk will get a more complex question than "Where is the toilet?" or "Can I borrow a stapler?" (Henry and Neville, 2008). But there is still scope for librarians to interact with users in the management, design, and arrangement of physical space. Indeed, this activity is a key part of the first law of the new librarian-ship—"libraries serve humanity" (Crawford and Gorman, 1995, p. 8). Li-brary spaces now need to serve users, rather than serving books or librarians.

It is true that librarianship as a profession has primarily focused on con-necting users with the right information (Dalrymple, 1984; Hjørland, 2000; Wolfe, Naylor, and Drueke, 2010). It is also true that librarians have, by default, been making decisions about physical spaces for as long as libraries have provided spaces to study and work—a very long time indeed. For many, librarianship in the twenty-first century will mean finding different ways to be a part of the information pipeline; however, some readers of this chapter may find more appeal in creating and managing physical spaces.

There is certainly plenty to do in this field: the concept of "learning spaces" is gaining more and more attention on campuses where in-person classes are held (Oblinger, 2006), and (as the authors have discovered in their own library) even online-only students sometimes come in to use the library's physical space. Librarians have been in charge of "learning spaces" since before they got their inverted commas, so they are well placed to contribute to the discussion and the discipline around them, provided they are willing to engage with and listen to the users of those spaces.

While the platonic archetype of a library is solo study carrels, perhaps with green glass lamps, things have changed, and libraries have to change to meet changing needs. Dana McKay and one of her colleagues recently completed an evaluation of the use of Swinburne's library space over the course of an entire academic term, including exams (McKay and Buchanan, 2014). They did not speak to students as part of this; instead, they observed how library spaces were being used, and counting things like group work and devices in use. This study was rounded out with some close observations of group work; solo study is fairly well understood, but group needs are still a bit of a mystery. Despite librarians being well positioned to do this study, it was in fact a pair of computer scientists that did the work—albeit computer scientists with an interest in how humans use technology.

In contrast to the romantic vision of solo scholars with green glass lamps, this study found that Swinburne Library is a hive of very modern activity (McKay and Buchanan, 2014). Yes, 7 percent of users were using books exclusively (a number that drops to 3 percent when examining people in groups), but 30 percent of people were working in groups, and 43 percent were using technology they had brought with them into the library.

One of the big changes in library space, then, is that the new library needs power, and lots of it. A number of students were seen carrying multiboxes so that they could power all their devices, and a single user identified, in an ad hoc conversation, six devices she was carrying that needed regular charging. No, twenty-first-century librarianship does not require an electrician's certification, but it does require an awareness of the devices users carry, the ways in which they use them, and the furniture required to support this. The particular configuration of devices and power is likely to vary, according to the user population at each library, and the landscape is changing. Foster's work (Foster and Gibbons, 2007) found only a minority of students carrying large, heavy, and expensive laptops to the library. McKay and Buchanan's study in 2014 suggests a shift.

The other big change from the traditional library to the modern library is the presence of group work, and the social and physical changes this imposes on a library. In terms of the social, there are conflicting pressures on libraries: some users want silent (or quiet) space to pursue solo work, and others want a place to meet and socialize. This has been seen repeatedly in studies of libraries (Bailin, 2011; Bryant, Matthews, and Walton, 2009; Foster and Gibbons, 2005), and local observations bear this out. The balance between social space and quiet space is probably wrong in Swinburne Library at present: silent spaces reached capacity long before group spaces (McKay and Buchanan, 2014). Without further investigation, this issue would not have become apparent: other libraries may well be different. This study also confirmed that user expectations are often not met, and like at least one library in the literature (Bryant, Matthews, and Walton, 2009), Swinburne Library users will not self-police quiet spaces. Librarians, particularly those who have worked in a number of libraries, are likely to be extremely well placed to analyze what works and what doesn't to create social norms around physical spaces.

In terms of the physical, the new discipline of learning spaces is largely focused on group learning spaces. Swinburne Library is fortunate to have a group learning space designed by educators (Lee, 2009) (see figures 8.2–8.4).

This space proved to work really well; it can be full to capacity without feeling overcrowded or chaotic. It does not meet all users' requirements, however: Swinburne Library also has a number of honeycomb-patterned desks with in situ desktop computers (see figure 8.5) that were commonly used by pairs to take advantage of the privacy afforded by the walls of the honeycomb, and the shared large display and computer.

Close examination of the data collected in this study reveals that laptops are private devices used only by their owners. This insight snapped into focus when the researchers observed the single incident of laptop sharing seen during the study; this sharing was akin to an act of intimacy. Nonetheless, the privacy of laptops is a hindrance to larger groups who want to both control their own laptops and share working: Large screens help for viewing, but do not allow shared control. Again, this is a norm in Swinburne Library (and one that is not supported by its physical spaces), but other libraries may be different.

Librarians' relationships with physical space are also changing. Librarians are no longer "shushers," and physical spaces are no longer merely conduits to information or silent asylums of private scholarly reflection. Just as librarians are trained to handle information, many experienced academic librarians will have insights into the management of the physical spaces that used to be so utterly inseparable from the information. These spaces remain a key part of the academic experience for many students, even if they are

Figure 8.2.   A range of table types in our dedicated group study area. *Image copyright 2014 Dana McKay*

getting their information from a screen. Ensuring that libraries—including their spaces—serve users, rather than the other way around, is a core principle on which librarians should act, now and in the future.

Figure 8.3. Round tables and a glass wall for writing on in dedicated group study area. *Image copyright 2014 Dana McKay*

R. E. S. P. E. C. T.

Understanding and respecting knowledge in all its forms is an expectation of the second law of new librarianship (Crawford and Gorman, 1995, p. 8). Many theorists have attempted to define knowledge, with varying degrees of success. Ackoff, cited in Rowley (2007), perhaps comes closest by arguing that there is a distinction between *data* (unprocessed symbols), *information* (data with meaning that becomes useful), *knowledge* (answers the "how" questions arising from information), and *wisdom* (understanding what adds value to knowledge). For a working definition, though, librarians might best be served by a view of knowledge as information filtered through the lens of individual values and experience (Davenport and Prusak, 2000)—information that is "actionable" (Jashapara, 2005, cited in Rowley, 2007).

The discipline of knowledge management is not new to librarians, although it perhaps hasn't played as strong a role in the past in academic libraries as it does in special and corporate libraries. Knowledge management theory operates on the assumption that there are (at least) two types of knowledge: tacit and explicit. By attempting to record the tacit knowledge

Figure 8.4.   Booth seating in group study area. *Image copyright 2014 Dana McKay*

that exists in the heads of a few, librarians can seek to make that knowledge explicit for the benefit of many. Some (Bocij et al., 2003) argue that it is impossible to make tacit knowledge explicit, while others believe that explicit knowledge is simply information repackaged (Rowley, 2007). Nevertheless, new tools targeting this outcome emerge all the time, and librarians in the twenty-first century can make a career from managing and manipulating these tools.

Intranets are used in many organizations to capture and communicate key information about the organization and its staff. Managing intranets, with their clear knowledge management impetus, is a good role for librarians keen to bring together their strengths in information organization, search engine optimization, document management, and digital literacy.

A more ubiquitous knowledge management tool is Wikipedia, which seeks to make the tacit knowledge of the world explicit in a free and open way. Wikipedia, like Google, is often dismissed by librarians, who lament the poor quality control of the resource and express concerns about its unguarded use by undergraduate students. Yet many Wikipedia articles are written by experts in the field, and/or by "other knowledgeable people to

Figure 8.5. "Honeycomb"-style computer seating. *Image copyright 2014 Dana McKay*

whom deference is paid" (Sanger, 2009). A 2005 *Nature* study (Giles, 2005) comparing Wikipedia against reference stalwart *Encyclopaedia Britannica* found that accuracy rates were much the same across both resources. So it is disingenuous to see a few poor articles in Wikipedia as representative of the whole.

Many galleries, museums, archives, and libraries have started taking on a "Wikipedian in residence" (Wikipedia, 2014), a role dedicated to improving relevant content on the online resource and to building long-term capability within the host institution. Wikipedia, like Google, is not an enemy unless librarians allow it to be. Rather, librarians can play an important role in ensuring that the information presented on Wikipedia is correct, up-to-date, and referenced properly. Parent organizations will appreciate librarians carrying out this work on their behalf to engender a positive representation of their public profile.

Philosopher Lawrence Sanger (2009) argues that the success of Wikipedia poses a challenge to traditional notions and hierarchies of knowledge, expertise, and power—though sadly this challenge is not yet being met (Lam, et al., 2011). As suggested in the second new law of library science (Crawford and Gorman, 1995, p. 8), an important ingredient of the new librarianship will be respect for the wisdom and abilities of others. Definitive texts on the practice of reference librarianship such as Katz (2002) give the reference librarian hero status and reinforce an air of academic superiority. This comes at the expense of library users, who are portrayed as bumbling fools who don't have a hope of finding the right answer because they don't know the right question to ask. This assertion, as well as being patronizing, ignores the failings of the systems libraries offer users (Borgman, 1996) and is demonstrably false anyway (McKay and Buchanan, 2013). These attitudes are the antithesis of a service culture, and they belong in the same day and age as a building that puts the librarian on a pedestal.

One of the authors of this chapter is not a librarian; however, she is an information specialist. As a user experience specialist, she was hired into a library to focus on what end users need, and to work out how to make it happen. Her role often means cutting through the kind of traditionalism that makes librarians afraid of Google, and that will, if librarians are not thoughtful and adaptive, spell the end of the profession. Librarianship as a profession must be realistic about the twenty-first-century information landscape. Users no longer require librarians as intermediaries between themselves and information; they can find things for themselves—a situation they prefer (Fast and Campbell, 2004)—and they often do a very good job (Brophy and Bawden, 2005). Bemoaning changes in the behavior of academic library user groups and the systems they prefer only serves to alienate users. Proving the value in academic libraries means setting aside the conventional approaches of the past, and embracing new ideas and professions.

COMPUTER SAYS YES

The other author of this chapter (who *is* a librarian) wrote a tongue-in-cheek article for her professional magazine in 2013 detailing why librarians need to stop fighting consumer technology and embrace it to build our services and remain relevant (Parker, 2013). The subject of the article was Google, but knowing when to "use technology intelligently to enhance service" (Crawford and Gorman, 1995, p. 8) is the principle behind the third law of the new librarianship.

The article observed that the expectations of librarians working in a university environment are growing alongside those of their users, and this includes expectations of search. There is in fact a serious side to the tension between librarians and Google. Librarians of the future (especially those who have worked in digital libraries) are in an excellent position to work in fields such as web and intranet content management that benefit greatly from search engine optimization. Librarians understand how search works, including the relatively invisible power of Boolean logic. The literature amply demonstrates that browse and search are not the same thing, but that they *are* overlapping information-seeking practices (Marchionini et al., 1993; Kuhlthau, 1999). Librarians also understand the value—and the art—of good metadata; thus, they can assist content owners with creating logical navigation structures and building successful content based on effective use of keywords. Librarians can do all these things, and do them well, but to be effective, the "them and us" dichotomy between Google and the librarian must be abandoned.

Google will only be an enemy of libraries as long as they are perceived as being in competition. Librarians spend a lot of time teaching users not to trust Google, yet are keen to implement discovery layers that are valued for their "Google-like" search. Why replicate the Google search experience instead of just making it work for libraries? Institutional repositories provide a clear business case for the value of teamwork between librarians and search engines. The research collections librarians curate through these tools are of great value to people all around the world, but librarians' roles in making them available should be almost invisible, and certainly seamless. Thanks to search engines, those interested in research findings worldwide should never have to know our repositories exist, because these hand-crafted collections are optimized for harvesting by Google, Google Scholar, and other services, which will be the entry point for the majority of users.

When promoting repository services to researchers, they always ask: "Is it in Google?" If the answer is no, repositories lose significant traction with academics seeking to boost their research profile, as well as an opportunity to prove the worth of libraries to their parent organizations. Google is always hungry for content, so librarians should be ready to feed it. Designing libraries with customers in mind means embracing, rather than rejecting, the technologies they know and love, especially where they actually serve libraries' own ends.

DIDN'T KNOW HOW LOST I WAS UNTIL I FOUND YOU

While users have become highly effective at meeting their own information needs and increasingly use information that is sourced online, there is a gap in online service provision, and it is one that users notice. That gap is browsing. Readers value the chance to find the things they didn't know they were looking for—the happy accident that constitutes serendipity.

In 2004, a librarian noted the changes that were coming in the transition to digital library services, and she said that serendipity was "too important to be left to chance" (Cooksey, 2004). And she's right. The flaws inherent in all the major classification schemes are manifold (as librarians know) and include their sometimes impenetrability to users (Gorman, 1981; McKay and Conyers, 2010). Nonetheless the experience of browsing the shelves is valued by users (Buchanan et al., 2005; Blandford, Rimmer, and Warwick, 2006; Hinze et al., 2012), and savvy users understand that this experience is not replicated online (Makri et al., 2007. Study after study shows users complaining that online books don't offer them the opportunity to browse, and that they miss it. For some users this is enough of a reason to avoid e-books entirely Hinze et al., 2012), which is a concern as library collections move increasingly online. This love affair with the shelves is backed up with hard evidence: In both 1993 (Hancock-Beaulieu, 1993) and 2008 (McKay, Smith, and Chang, 2014), co-located books were often borrowed together. Over half of all library users who found one book on the shelves in 1993 also selected another (Hancock-Beaulieu, 1993); in 2013 the same proportion of library users stated that browsing was an important part of their book-seeking process (Kleiner, Rädle, and Reiterer, 2013).

Browsing is a core part of the human information-seeking process (Kuhlthau, 1999)—it can work in tandem with search, or it can be a strategy in its own right. The gains readers make from browsing are not, at this stage, entirely clear in the literature, though the profession does have some ideas. Nonbibliographic cues—such as book size (Thudt, Hinrichs, and Carpendale, 2012), dust (Stelmaszewska and Blandford, 2002), and number of copies (Makri et al., 2007)—help readers determine book relevance for their particular needs, yet catalogs usually only offer bibliographic details (Borgman, 1996). Well-versed users understand that shelf location in and of itself may be a relevance cue (Makri et al., 2007).

The most frequently mentioned benefit of the shelves, though, is the joy of finding the perfect thing without looking: serendipity (Stelmaszewska & Blandford, 2002; Blandford, Rimmer, and Warwick, 2006; Makri et al., 2007; Hinze et al., 2012; Saarti, 1997). Shelves offer this because they are physical in some ways: readers spy something on the way to the toilet (Hinze et al., 2012), or check the things others have recently returned (Ooi, 2008; Saarinen and Vakkari, 2013). The shelves also offer readers the ability to ease into examining books—first touching them, then half removing them, then taking them completely off the shelves—all while retaining the ability to see alternative books at a glance. This behavior closely matches the definition of browsing Bates (2007) gives; this definition is grounded in human psychology. The shelves are not perfect, however—books can only exist in one place on the shelves (even if they fit neatly into two topics), and users are annoyed by missing, mis-shelved, or loaned books (Blandford, Rimmer, and Warwick, 2006). The move to online materials has the potential to make users happier *if* their browsing needs can be met.

Computer science as a discipline "gets" that readers want to browse: A number of test systems have come out recently that replicate shelves on a large display (Kleiner, Rädle, and Reiterer, 2013), allow users to drag sliders around to explore a book collection (Pearce and Chang, 2014), or give users "fun" browsing tools such as color sorting and size-sorting books (Thudt, Hinrichs, and Carpendale, 2012). Users like these systems, but they are trial systems, and not grounded in a rigorous requirements-gathering process. Librarians have known for decades that users like to browse, and some libraries now offer online browsing systems.[1] These systems, though, are (again) not grounded in a rigorous understanding of what browsing means.

Librarians have something special to bring to the creation of online browsing. Astute users understand that the shelves are organized by librarians and appreciate this, claiming it as a unique information experience. Librarians, who understand classification systems, should take an active interest in developing such systems—though this exercise must also respect and leverage the expertise of partners in technology, human computer interaction, and design. Librarians should also support any online system that aggregates usage data to provide recommendations for end users, as far as is legally possible. Finally, librarians can be a source of serendipity too: passing along a recommendation of what to read next to a familiar user (when librarians themselves have that "aha" moment) will be experienced as serendipity, provided the recommendation is useful.

Serendipity is too important to be left to chance, and librarians have a clear role in supporting both people and technology to ensure it is not lost.

I WANT TO BREAK FREE

How best to use technology to enhance library services is an open question, and it will remain so as technology evolves. Crawford and Gorman's (1995) fourth law—"protect access to knowledge" (p. 8)—has been very warmly embraced by a generation of modern librarians. Many librarians have strong libertarian views on open access that help drive the development of ambitious information policy.

There have been a number of attacks on openness over the past five years. In 2012, the United States Congress nearly passed the Research Works Act,[2] a bill with the aim of crushing open-access mandates for federally funded research. Libraries, open-access groups, and academics spoke out against the bill, and Elsevier withdrew its support for the legislation. In the same year, the UK Working Group on Expanding Access to Published Research Findings released the Finch Report (2012), a guide to how the United Kingdom could make more research freely available online.

While any initiative to expand access to scholarly information should be applauded, the Finch Report made a misstep by recommending the expensive "gold" option, where authors pay a fee to publish their articles in an open-access journal, or more frequently a subscription journal with a paid open-access option. This kind of open access isn't free: it just shifts the cost of publishing from one group to another—in this case, from publishers back to authors, and also to the taxpayers who fund research grants. It also allows publishers to hold academic research ransom. For all research content to be available through gold open access, UK research funders would need to direct a large percentage of existing funding toward publishing articles, instead of funding the research that fuels them. Librarians responded to this dilemma by highlighting that there is a cheaper alternative: authors can deposit publisher-approved versions of their papers into open-access repositories. Again, librarians were at the vanguard, waving the flag and ensuring that the movement continued. It is important to maintain this role as advocates of open access to information, now and into the future.

Corporate information management by its nature involves protecting some information from a public audience, for example where it contains commercially valuable or sensitive information. This doesn't mean that librarians can't make open-access principles apply on at least a local level when establishing information policy within universities. Librarians who have been working in repositories and scholarly publishing for a while will be familiar with the challenges of making material open. Yet the problem within organizations is quite different. The first difficulty, before dealing with mixed attitudes toward openness, is that the material simply isn't digital or accessible in the first place. Many information professionals express concern about transitioning to online-only information due to the risk of technology and format obsolescence. While this is a very real concern, there are mitigation strategies available, such as using open standards and common archival formats. By contrast, managing corporate information in paper form is costly and volatile. In the event of fire or flood, there is no offsite backup copy for paper information—the files are simply gone.

Librarians can play an important role in ensuring that corporate information—from the most ephemeral documents to the most significant artifacts—is well-maintained, discoverable, and accessible now and into the future.

HONORING THE PAST AND CREATING THE FUTURE

As this chapter demonstrates, academic libraries have been evolving and changing for decades, sometimes without anyone noticing. Information is increasingly online and open to all, spaces are flexible and user-centered, and the reference desk is quiet. But what is perhaps more interesting is that librarians have been changing too. Ranganathan's laws set the standard in the last century, but the twenty-first-century librarian has a new manifesto, created by Crawford and Gorman in 1995. The laws of library science for the modern librarian focus on new information delivery methods, strengthen the role of technology in the practice of modern librarianship, and offer the opportunity to take these skills into new domains. In short, librarianship has extended far beyond the walls of the library.

There will always be a place for people willing to take on a challenge. One of the biggest challenges humans face in the modern age is information chaos: the amount of information available (such as the three hundred hours of video uploaded to YouTube every minute)[3] increasingly exceeds a human's ability to even understand what is there. This is a problem for all information seekers, and increasingly it is seen as a critical risk to organizations as they lose sight of their valuable corporate information in the morass. Information is the core business of universities, however they are not always very good at looking after it. Putting some order around information chaos is a time-honored role for librarians; modern technology offers both the opportunity to do this in novel ways and the requirement that *someone* does it. Universities are looking to librarians to occupy this space, and taking up roles outside the traditional remit of librarianship will enable the profession to extend the reach of librarianship into the future.

There will always be a role for critical thinkers who understand and respect information in all its forms. Ensuring equitable access to information while respecting and valuing creators is a key pillar of library philosophy, and it will remain so in the future. Technology both enables this respectful sharing and impedes it: information can be transferred cheaply, and there is no technological limitation on the number of users accessing a single document at the same time. Conversely, in the escalating war between publishers and consumers, ever-stricter controls are put in place to protect business models that have no place in the age of technology,[4] and (some) consumers flout the right of creators to be paid for and receive credit for their work. The modern librarian has a place in all this, guiding policy and supporting consumers in their quest for fair access to content.

In this chapter, the authors have gazed into the crystal ball and found that the future looks very different for libraries. But are librarians an endangered species? Is this the end of the world as we know it? The authors don't think so—at least not yet. Librarianship has weathered many a meteor shower, so extinction is far from a given. Complacency is the enemy of librarianship practice, though, because academic libraries are being challenged by their parent organizations, and users are finding new ways of navigating information without help. Librarianship in the twenty-first century will need new skills and new ideas. Because there will only be a role for librarians of the future if it is accepted that what was once the "scary library" is now just "the library." Provided librarians can accept this, extend their knowledge to the places where information skills are useful, and look at work with a user-centered lens, they'll be fine.

The authors would like to thank Dr. George Buchanan of City University London for thought-provoking discussions about the future of libraries that helped shape this chapter. Rebecca Parker would like to thank Derek White-head and Teula Morgan of Swinburne University of Technology for encouraging her to explore what a librarian is, or might be.

NOTES

1. See for example WhichBook, http://www.openingthebook.com/whichbook/, and University of Technology Sydney's shelf view http://www.lib.uts.edu.au/news/92740/another-new-way-to-browse-librarys-collection.
2. Research Works Act, H.R. 3699 (December 16, 2011).
3. http://www.youtube.com/yt/press/statistics.html
4. For a good example of librarian advocacy on technology and consumer rights see Sarah Houghton's "Ebook User's Bill of Rights," http://librarianinblack.net/librarianinblack/ebookrights/.

REFERENCES

Bailin, K. 2011. "Changes in Academic Library Space: A Case Study at the University of New South Wales." *Australian Academic and Research Libraries* 42 (4): 342–59.
Bates, M. J. 2007. "What Is Browsing Really? A Model Drawing from Behavioural Science Research." *Information Research* 12 (4).
Blandford, A., J. Rimmer, and C. Warwick. 2006. "Experiences of the Library in the Digital Age." In *Proceedings of the 3rd International Conference on Cultural Convergence and Digital Technology, Athens, Greece, 23–25 November 2006.* Tavros, Greece: Foundation of the Hellenic World.
Bocij, P., D. Chaffey, A. Greasley, and S. Hickie. 2003. *Business Information Systems: Technology, Development and Management for the E-business.* Harlow, UK: Financial Times/Prentice Hall.
Borgman, C. L. 1996. "Why Are Online Catalogs Still Hard to Use?" *Journal of the American Society for Information Science* 47 (7): 493–503.
Brodie, M. 2008. "Watch This Space! Designing a New Library for Macquarie University." In *Proceedings of the VALA 14th Biennial Conference and Exhibition (VALA 2008), Melbourne, 5–7 February 2008.* Melbourne: VALA.
Brophy, J., and D. Bawden. 2005. "Is Google Enough? Comparison of an Internet Search Engine with Academic Library Resources." *ASLIB Proceedings: New Information Perspectives* 57 (6): 498–512.
Bryant, J., G. Matthews, and G. Walton. 2009. "Academic Libraries and Social and Learning Space." *Journal of Librarianship and Information Science*, 41 (1): 7–18.
Buchanan, G., S. J. Cunningham, A. Blandford, J. Rimmer, and C. Warwick. 2005. "Information Seeking by Humanities Scholars." In *Proceedings of the 9th European Conference on Digital Libraries, Vienna, 18–23 September 2005,* 218–229. Berlin: Springer.
Cain, S. 2013. *Quiet: The Power of Introverts in a World That Can't Stop Talking.* New York: Random House.
Clark, A. V. H. 2014. "Transferable Skills: From Rocks to Books." In *Skills to Make a Librarian: Transferable Skills Inside and Outside the Library,* edited by D. Lowe-Wincentsen, 11–20. Oxford: Chandos.
Cooksey, E. B. 2004. "Too Important to Be Left to Chance: Serendipity and the Digital Library." *Science and Technology Libraries* 25 (1–2): 23–32.

Crabtree, A., M. B. Twidale, J. O'Brien, and D. M. Nichols. 1997. "Talking in the Library: Implications for the Design of Digital Libraries." In *Proceedings of the 2nd International ACM Conference on Digital Libraries, Philadelphia, United States, 23–26 July 1997*, 221–28. New York: ACM.

Crawford, W., and M. Gorman. 1995. *Future Libraries: Dreams, Madness and Reality*. Chicago: American Library Association.

Dalrymple, P. W. 1984. "Closing the Gap: The Role of the Librarian in Online Searching." *RQ* 24 (2): 177–85.

Davenport, T. H., and L. Prusak. 2000. *Working Knowledge: How Organizations Manage What They Know*. Boston: Harvard Business School Press.

Edquist, H. 2013. *A New World: Celebrating the Dome*. State Library of Victoria. Accessed February 1, 2015. http://exhibitions.slv.vic.gov.au/node/15432.

Fast, K. V., and D. G. Campbell. 2004. "'I Still Like Google': University Student Perceptions of Searching OPACs and the Web." *Proceedings of the American Society for Information Science and Technology* 41 (1): 138–46.

Federation of Enterprise Architecture Professional Organizations. 2013. *A Common Perspective on Enterprise Architecture*. The Federation of Enterprise Architecture Professional Organizations.

Foster, N. F., and S. Gibbons. 2005. "Understanding Faculty to Improve Content Recruitment for Institutional Repositories." *D-Lib Magazine* 11 (1).

———. 2007. *Studying Students: The Undergraduate Research Project at the University of Rochester*. Chicago: Association of College and Research Libraries.

Fulton, J. A. 2005. "Common Information Model." In *Encyclopedia of Database Technologies and Applications*, edited by L. C. Rivero, J. H. Doorn, and V. E. Ferraggine, 78–86. Hershey, PA: Idea Group.

Giles, J. (2005). "Internet Encyclopaedias Go Head to Head." *Nature* 438 (December 15): 900–901.

Gorman, M. 1981. "The Longer the Number the Smaller the Spine." *American Libraries* 12 (8): 498.

Hahn, K. 2009. "Introduction: Positioning Liaison Librarians for the 21st Century." *Research Library Issues: A Bimonthly Report from ARL, CNI, and SPARC*, no. 265 (August), pp. 1–2.

Hancock-Beaulieu, M. 1993. "Evaluating the Impact of an Online Library Catalogue on Subject Searching at the Catalogue and at the Shelves." *Journal of Documentation* 46 (4): 318–38.

Henry, D. B., and T. M. Neville. 2008. "Testing Classification Systems for Reference Questions." *Reference & User Services Quarterly* 47 (4): 364–73.

Hines, S. S. 2013. "What Will Libraries Be When They Grow Up? Responding to the Innovations of Technology and Imagining the Future." In *Imagine, Innovate, Inspire: The Proceedings of the ACRL 2013 Conference*, edited by D. M. Mueller, 638–42. Chicago: ACRL.

Hinze, A., D. McKay, N. Vanderschantz, C. Timpany, and S. J. Cunningham. 2012. "Book Selection Behavior in the Physical Library: Implications for Ebook Collections." In *Proceedings of the 12th ACM/IEEE-CS Joint Conference on Digital Libraries (JCDL 2012), Washington, DC, United States, 10–14 June 2012*, 305–14. New York: ACM.

Hjørland, B. 2000. "Library and Information Science: Practice, Theory, and Philosophical Basis." *Information Processing and Management* 36 (3): 501–31.

International Institute of Business Analysis. 2009. *A Guide to the Business Analysis Body of Knowledge (BABOK Guide), Version 2.0*. Toronto: The International Institute of Business Analysis.

Jashapara, A. 2005. *Knowledge Management: An Integrated Approach*. Harlow, UK: Financial Times/Prentice Hall.

Katz, W. A. 2002. *Introduction to Reference Work, Vol. 1: Basic Information Services* (8th ed.). New York: McGraw Hill.

Kleiner, E., R. Rädle, and H. Reiterer. 2013. Blended Shelf: Reality-Based Presentation and Exploration of Library Collections. In *Proceedings of the SIGCHI Conference on Human Factors in Computing Systems (CHI 2013), Paris, France, 27 April–2 May 2013*, 577–82. New York: ACM.

Koppi, T., L. Bogle, and N. Lavitt. 2004. "Institutional Use of Learning Objects: Lessons Learned and Future Directions." *Journal of Educational Multimedia and Hypermedia* 13 (4): 449–63.

Kuhlthau, C. C. 1999. "Inside the Search Process: Information Seeking from the User's Perspective." *Journal of the American Society for Information Science and Technology* 42 (5): 361–71.

Lam, S. K., A. Uduwage, Z. Dong, S. Sen, D. R Musicant, L Terveen, et al. (2011). "WP: Clubhouse? An Exploration of Wikipedia's Gender Imbalance." In *Proceedings of the 7th International Symposium on Wikis and Open Collaboration, Mountain View, United States, 3–5 October 2011*, 1–10. New York: ACM.

Lee, N. 2009. "The Hawthorn Project Hub at Swinburne University of Technology." In *Proceedings of the 2008 Next Generation Learning Spaces Colloquium, Brisbane, Australia, 1–2 October 2008*, 81–84. St. Lucia, Australia: University of Queensland.

LousyLibrarian. 2015. *Twitter Status: LousyLibrarian*. January 8. Accessed February 1, 2015, from Twitter: https://twitter.com/lousylibrarian/status/552841681327108097.

Makri, S., A. Blandford, J. Gow, J. Rimmer, C. Warwick, and G. Buchanan. 2007. "A Library or Just Another Information Resource? A Case Study of Users' Mental Models of Traditional and Digital Libraries." *Journal of the American Society for Information Science and Technology* 58 (3): 433–45.

Mann, T. (2008). "The Peloponnesian War and the Future of Reference, Cataloging, and Scholarship in Research Libraries." *Journal of Library Metadata* 8 (1): 53–100.

Marchionini, G., S. Dwiggins, A. Katz, and X. Lin. 1993. "Information Seeking in Full-Text End-User-Oriented Search Systems: The Roles of Domain and Search Expertise." *Library and Information Science Research* 15 (1): 35–69.

Martell, C. 2007. "The Elusive User: Changing Use Patterns in Academic Libraries 1995 to 2004." *College & Research Libraries* 68 (5): 435–45.

McKay, D., and G. Buchanan. 2013. "Boxing Clever: How Searchers Use and Adapt to a One-Box Library Search." In *Proceedings of OZCHI 2013, Adelaide, Australia, 25–29 November 2013*, 497–506. New York: ACM.

———. 2014. "On the Other Side from You: How Library Design Facilitates and Hinders Group Work." In *Proceedings of the 26th Australian Computer-Human Interaction Conference on Designing Futures, Sydney, 2–5 December 2014*, 97–106. New York: ACM.

McKay, D., and B. Conyers. 2010. "Where The Streets Have No Name: How Library Users Get Lost in the Stacks." In *Proceedings of the 11th Annual ACM SIGCHI NZ Conference on Computer-Human Interaction (CHINZ 2010), Auckland, New Zealand, 8–9 July 2010*, 77–80. New York: ACM.

McKay, D., W. Smith, and S. Chang. 2014. "Lend Me Some Sugar: Borrowing Rates of Neighbouring Books as Evidence for Browsing." In *Proceedings of the 2014 Joint Conference on Digital Libraries, London, 8–12 September 2014*, 145–54. Piscataway, NJ: IEEE.

Myburgh, S., and A. M. Tammaro. 2013. *Exploring Education for Digital Librarians: Meaning, Modes and Models*. Oxford: Chandos.

Nordlie, R. 1999. "'User Revealment': A Comparison of Initial Queries and Ensuing Question Development in Online Searching and in Human Reference Interactions." In *Proceedings of the 22nd Annual ACM Conference on Research and Development in Information Retrieval, Berkeley, CA, United States, 15–19 August 1999*, 11–18. New York: ACM.

Oblinger, D. G. 2006. *Learning Spaces*. Washington, DC: EDUCAUSE.

Ooi, K. 2008. "How Adult Fiction Readers Select Fiction Books in Public Libraries: A Study of Information Seeking in Context." Unpublished master of library and information studies thesis, Wellington, New Zealand, Victoria University of Wellington.

Parker, R. 2008. "Beyond the Holy Grail: Why Academic Librarianship Is More Than Just Reference." In *4th ALIA New Librarians Symposium (NLS4), Melbourne, Victoria, Australia, 5–6 December 2008*. Deakin, Australia: ALIA.

———. 2013. "Know Thy Frenemy? Thank Google for Repositories." *Incite* 34 (6–7): 21.

Pearce, J., and S. Chang. 2014. "Exploration without Keywords: The Bookfish Case." In *Proceedings of the 26th Australian Computer-Human Interaction Conference (OzCHI 2014), Sydney, Australia, 2–5 December 2014*, 76–79. New York: ACM.

Quirolgico, S., P. Assis, A. Westerinen, M. Baskey, and E. Stokes. 2004. "Toward a Formal Common Information Model Ontology." In *Proceedings of the WISE 2004 International Workshops, Brisbane, 22–24 November 2004*, edited by C. Bussler, S.-k. Hong, W. Jun, R. Kaschek, Kinshuk, S. Krishnaswamy, et al., 11–21. Berlin: Springer.

Ranganathan, S. R. 1931. *The Five Laws of Library Science*. Madras: The Madras Library Association.

Rowley, J. 2007. "The Wisdom Hierarchy: Representations of the DIKW Hierarchy." *Journal of Information Science* 33 (2): 163–80.

Saarinen, K., and P. Vakkari, P. 2013. "A Sign of a Good Book: Readers' Methods of Accessing Fiction in the Public Library." *Journal of Documentation* 69 (5): 736–54.

Saarti, J. (1997). "Feeding with the Spoon, or the Effects of Shelf Classification of Fiction on the Loaning of Fiction." *Information Services and Use* 17 (2–3): 159.

Sanger, L. M. (2009). "The Fate of Expertise after Wikipedia." *Episteme* 6 (1): 52–73.

Sessions, R. (2007). *A Comparison of the Top Four Enterprise-Architecture Methodologies*. Microsoft Developer Network Library. Accessed February 8, 2015. https://msdn.microsoft.com/en-us/library/bb466232.aspx.

Stelmaszewska, H., and A. Blandford. 2002. "Patterns of Interactions: User Behaviour in Response to Search Results." In *Proceedings of the JCDL 2002 Workshop on Usability of Digital Libraries, Portland, Oregon, 14–18 July 2002*, edited by A. Blandford, and G. Buchanan, 29–32. London: UCL Interaction Centre.

———. 2004. "From Physical to Pigital: A Case Study of Computer Scientists' Behaviour in Physical Libraries." *International Journal on Digital Libraries* 4 (2): 82–92.

Talja, S., and H. Maula. 2003. "Reasons for the Use and Non-use of Electronic Journals and Databases: A Domain Analytic Study in Four Scholarly Disciplines." *Journal of Documentation* 59 (6): 673–91.

Tenopir, C., D. W. King, S. Edwards, and L. Wu. 2009. "Electronic Journals and Changes in Scholarly Article Seeking and Reading Patterns." *ASLIB Proceedings* 61 (1): 5–32.

Thudt, A., U. Hinrichs, and S. Carpendale. 2012. "The Bohemian Bookshelf: Supporting Serendipitous Book Discoveries through Information Visualization." In *Proceedings of the SIGCHI Conference on Human Factors in Computing Systems, Austin, Texas, 5–12 May 2012*, 1461–70. New York: ACM.

UK Working Group on Expanding Access to Published Research Findings. 2012. *Accessibility, Sustainability, Excellence: How to Expand Access to Research Publications*. London: UK Government.

Weinberger, D. 2007. *Everything Is Miscellaneous: The Power of the New Digital Disorder*. New York: Times Books.

Whitehead, D. 2010. "Liaison 2015 at Swinburne." Presented at Capabilities for the 21st Century Library Part I: CAVAL Reference Interest Group Forum, 20 May 2010, Bundoora, Australia.

Wikipedia. (2014). "Wikipedian in Residence." Wikipedia. Accessed February 8, 2015. http://en.wikipedia.org/wiki/Wikipedian_in_residence.

Wilson, T. C. 1998. *The Systems Librarian: Designing Roles, Defining Skills*. Chicago: American Library Association.

Wolfe, J. A., T. Naylor, and J. Drueke, J. 2010. "The Role of the Academic Reference Librarian in the Learning Commons." *Reference and User Services Quarterly* 50 (2): 108–13.

Chapter Nine

Embedded Librarians

Case Studies from Loyola University, New Orleans

Teri Gallaway, Elizabeth Kelly, Brian Sullivan, and Malia Willey

The concept and practice of embedded librarianship has no dearth of definitions, articles, and case studies available for interested parties to consult. Case studies on embedded librarianship range from the successful, and sometimes not so successful, inclusion of librarians into classroom, online, residential, cocurricular, and other experiences. While embedded librarianship has evolved over the past few decades, there are core characteristics that remain consistent. For that reason, embedded librarianship is defined in this chapter's literature review as any experience that integrates a librarian into the environment of the users, allowing librarians to further connect with users. Librarians at the J. Edgar and Louise S. Monroe Library (Monroe Library), Loyola University, New Orleans (Loyola) have embedded in a variety of courses, including Historical Methods Lab, Interdisciplinary Humanities Research for honors students, Introduction to Music Industry Studies, and Synoptic Gospels.

This chapter provides a dual focus on the concept and practices of embedding librarians into courses. The chapter begins with a literature review, brief history, and characteristics of embedded librarianship, and is followed by case studies on embedded librarianship at the Monroe Library. The case studies provide readers with examples to apply at their home institutions.

LITERATURE REVIEW

"Embedded librarianship" is a relatively new phrase, but as a concept it stems from work being done by librarians for nearly a century. This work originated with branch libraries, small collections gathered by teaching faculty that were eventually compiled into formal collections (Drewes and Hoffman, 2010, p. 77). Librarians for these organizations were primarily responsible for collection development rather than for instruction or services. Branch libraries were, and still are, generally located within the same space as their user communities, and are therefore "at the forefront of discussions around education and services." Unfortunately, those piecemeal attempts at providing scholarly materials were not sustainable for most institutions (Hines, 2013, p. 2). Between World War I and World War II, libraries became more centralized and professional librarians were put in charge of resources. While this led to better access and bibliographic control, the physical movement of collection managers away from their user communities isolated librarians from their users. Still, the concept of the librarian working beyond the library extended to the realm of health care, where clinical medical librarians began joining physicians during rounds as early as the 1960s, with the practice becoming prevalent in the 1970s (Drewes and Hoffman, 2010, p. 77). In addition to locating the librarian where the greatest need for their service is, "becoming more user-centric by bringing library services to the user is one approach to decreasing financial support for the library" (Kenefick, 2011, p. 196). Simultaneously, the decline of the branch library led to a new concept, that of the liaison librarian (Hines, 2013, p. 3). Just as branch faculty/librarians worked with specific areas of study, library liaisons in higher education traditionally work with certain disciplines to support instruction and collection needs. In medical librarianship specifically, an increase in the literature in the 1980s about the impact of new technologies led from librarian focus on subject expertise toward better development of instructional skills (Martin, 2013, p. 252). Collaboration between faculty and libraries on instructional matters was advocated in a 1988 article by Rom and Lantz about art students (which also first coined the phrase "embedded librarian"), but it wasn't until the 1990s that a more holistic approach to integrating information literacy skills into curricular instruction began, in large part because of widespread adoption of the Internet (Hines, 2013, p. 5). By 1993, corporate librarians were trying to "get out of the library, and into the business" as well as "actively assess who needs information, and who has it—then help them to connect" (Shumaker, 2012a, p. 32). Finally, the term "embedded librarian" became prevalent in 2004 with Barbara Dewey's "The Embedded Librarian: Strategic Campus Collaborations" and other articles (Hines, 2013, p. 4).

The terminology originates with embedded journalists in the Iraq war (Dewey, 2004, p. 5). These journalists were integrated into military units "to observe and report on conflicts, exercises, and missions from an insider's vantage point" (Drewes and Hoffman, 2010, p. 76). Similarly, embedded librarians should mimic as closely as possible the environment of their users. The opportunities for librarians embedding are vast, varied, continually developing, and may fluctuate depending on the nature of the library and its user group. As such, the professional literature defines embedded librarians in many ways.

Higher education dominates the professional literature on embedding in academic libraries, despite the fact that less than a third of embedded librarians work in higher education (Shumaker, 2012a, p. 32). In academic libraries, librarians may embed throughout the college or university. Several studies have been done to determine activities common to embedded librarians. David Shumaker and Mary Talley received a 2007 Special Libraries Association (SLA) grant to study the qualities that make an embedded librarian program successful (Talley, 2011, p. 5). They administered a web-based survey of SLA members to determine a subset of embedded librarians. The qualified embedded librarians were then surveyed on the longevity and growth of the programs they worked in. The researchers finally made four site visits to two higher education and two for-profit organizations to perform in-depth interviews with staff and users (Shumaker and Talley, 2010, p. 27–28). One of the outcomes of the project was a classification of activities common to embedded librarians (Shumaker and Talley, 2009, p. 5–6). Similar results were found in a 2012 review of case studies (Schulte, 2012, p. 125) as well as in individual case studies and literature reviews. Some common activities of embedded librarians include:

- Embedding in course management systems (Schulte, 2012; Tumbleson and Burke, 2010; Yorke and Vance, 2009; Brower, 2011; Wu, Betts, Jacob, Nollan, and Norris, 2013; Knight and Loftis, 2012; Guillot, Stahr, and Meeker, 2010)
- Monitoring and participating in social media and other virtual environments (Hamilton, 2012; Brower, 2011)
- Collaborating with teaching faculty on course and/or assignment design (Schulte, 2012; Brower, 2011)
- Co-teaching courses, either online or face-to-face (Schulte, 2012; Shumaker, 2009; Kelly, 2008; Brower, 2011)
- Assisting students with in-depth research (Schulte, 2012)
- Assisting customers with in-depth research (Schulte, 2012)
- Physical location near user community (Schulte, 2012; Brower, 2011)
- Embedding within a college faculty (Doerksen, 2013)
- Working within research teams as a full participant (McCluskey, 2013)

Within higher education, librarians can even be embedded in activities that are not strictly academic, such as in student activities (Hines, 2013, p. 6) or in student dorms (Long, 2011). The literature contains many examples of the above-named activities. However, embedded librarians can also be found doing additional kinds of work within nonacademic organizations, including:

Health Libraries

- Attending grand rounds (Martin, 2013; Kenefick, 2011; Brower, 2011)
- Attending shift changes (Shumaker, 2009)
- Participating in research teams (Martin, 2013)
- Providing research services within community groups (Martin, 2013)
- Participating in grant applications (Kenefick, 2011; Federer, 2013a)
- Creating lending journal clubs (Kenefick, 2011)
- Providing instruction to medical professional staff (Kenefick, 2011)

Special Libraries

- Embedded in offices (Shumaker, 2009; Brower, 2011)

Public Libraries

- Providing research services within community groups (Shumaker, 2009)

As instruction has moved online through distance learning services, embedded librarians have also been integrating into online classes (Hines, 2013, p. 6). "Embedded librarian" is used frequently in the literature to specifically describe librarians working within content management systems, and this disparity in definition extends beyond the online versus face-to-face (Schulte, 2012, p. 122). Both Schulte and Shumaker/Talley found little difference in the work performed by self-identified embedded librarians and supposedly non-embedded librarians. It is difficult, therefore, to truly track the literature regarding methods and outcomes of information literacy instruction due to the surplus of ways in which the roles of information literacy practitioners can be described. Many of the activities listed above are undertaken by professionals who define themselves as course, personal, and lurking librarians (Yorke and Vance, 2009, p. 198); program analysts, information specialists, intelligence analysts, and information technology staff (Shumaker, 2012a, p. 34); blended, liaison, instructional design, and user experience librarians, or even informationists (Bell, 2013, p. xi; Federer, 2013b). In addition, the broad range of activities undertaken by embedded librarians lends to a diverse professional literature that can make the concept difficult to define (Drewes and Hoffman, 2010, p. 75).

Dewey (2004) asks, "Is the library as a physical space relevant to the embedded librarian concept?" (6). We have already seen the library move from within academic departments to a more centralized location, and now librarians are once again moving away from the library building to more proactively meet users. While it is not necessary for librarians to physically or metaphorically (in the case of online programs) relocate to where their users are, physical proximity helps make the librarian seem more like part of the user's community (Drewes and Hoffman, 2010, p. 76). Whether an embedded librarian is found in the library, a business office, in an online course, or in a hospital, perhaps what is most important is that the librarian becomes "an integral part to the whole" of their organization, as embedded librarianship is defined by Jezmynne Dene (Shumaker 2012b, p. 24–25). Another way to categorize embedded librarians is that traditionally, reference librarians were in a passive role, waiting for users to ask for help; now, embedded librarians try to anticipate the needs of their users (p. 27).

The literature indicates numerous benefits associated with embedded librarianship. Librarians have been traditionally associated with the physical library (Shumaker, 2012b). The embedded librarianship model turns librarians from an inward focus on the library and related services toward an outward focus on their user community and partnerships. Dewey (2004) emphasizes the importance of collaboration: "Innovative and exciting collaborations account for a major part of the library's transition from passive to active, reactive to proactive, staid to lively, and singular to social" (p. 6). Embedded librarians develop deeper collaborations with their institutions, which makes the library a more integral part of the community. In turn, library services become more aligned with the organization.

Some of the advantages reported from an embedded librarian experience include increased visibility, further engagement in the classroom, and a more informed understanding of the librarian's work and the work of other departments (Doerksen, 2013). The expertise of the librarian becomes more visible as personalized services are developed for users (Mon and Harris, 2011). This visibility is especially apparent in the classroom. One embedded librarian states, "Libraries benefit by gaining librarians with teaching faculty perspective; academic departments benefit from gaining library perspective; both benefit by building bridges between them; and ultimately students benefit from a more diverse range of faculty and a more cohesive delivery of the educational mission" (Doerksen, 2013, p. 82). When an embedded librarian co-teaches with another instructor, both instructors benefit from their mutual feedback, which may lead to improved course design (Kelly, 2008). Closer proximity to the institutional community allows for an improved understanding of users (Drewes and Hoffman, 2010). Librarians better understand the culture and meet the needs of their users through increased integration and interaction (Kenefick, 2011).

Embedded librarianship is not without challenges. Time constraints and time management concerns are predominant deterrents (Doerksen, 2013; Shumaker, 2009). In their examination of the pros and cons of different modes of information literacy instruction, however, Tumbleson and Burke (2010) conclude that "embedded librarian programs make the most sense and cents for investment of instruction librarian's time, training, and creative efforts" (p. 235) when compared to reference services, singular instruction sessions, credit courses, and library websites. While the availability of time is a challenge for librarians, an embedded librarian experience can be a strategic investment of time.

Some of the challenges reported from an embedded librarian experience include a heavier workload, the increased necessity to stay informed in new subject areas, and the need for acceptance from other faculty and administrators (Doerksen, 2013). Hawes (2011) reports on a successful embedded experience that required numerous pitches to gain administrator approval. As librarians become more involved in their user communities, the need to serve both the interests of their library and their users becomes more pronounced. While these demands may often overlap, Doerksen (2013) refers to this dichotomy as the challenge to "serve two masters" (p. 82).

Assessment remains another challenge for embedded librarianship. Schulte (2012) reports in her examination of the literature "Overall there is a lack of formal, systematic processes to quantify outcomes demonstrating embedded librarian impact" (p. 134). While many essays and case studies espouse the benefits of an embedded librarian experience, quality research studies on the topic, especially in the area of the evaluation of outcomes, are scarce. The diversity of experiences could explain the lack of cohesive assessment of embedded librarianship. Shumaker (2012b) proposes creating and applying a framework to evaluate the success of an embedded librarian program. Li (2012) and Helms and Whitesell (2013) report embedded librarian involvement in planning and achieving student learning facilitates the assessment of student learning outcomes. Assessment measures in online embedded experiences have included optional evaluations, which usually result in low response rates, and anonymous pre-tests and post-tests (Wu, Betts, Jacobs, Nollan, and Norris, 2013, p. 325).

There are several best practices related to embedded librarianship. Potential candidates for an embedded librarian experience should demonstrate a cultural readiness. The organization must be open to new experiences that may lead to greater success, and the embedded librarians should exhibit interpersonal skills, flexibility, and credibility within the targeted subject area (Shumaker 2009). Drewes and Hoffman (2010) summarize: "Key concepts for successful programs include location, communication, services, flexibility of librarians, and collaborations among librarians, faculty, staff, researchers, and students" (p. 81). Heider (2010) expands upon these best practices by emphasizing stakeholder buy-in and involvement as well as advocating full immersion with departmental activities including physical presence, collection development, and even publishing with departmental faculty.

Effective embedded librarian experiences share several characteristics. Indicators of success include a growth in the number of embedded librarian experiences, an increased demand for library services, and the development of new library services (Shumaker and Talley, 2010). Marketing and promotion, value-added services, evaluation, and management support are broad themes that occur in the successful experiences of embedded librarians (Shumaker, 2011). Embedded librarianship can be marketed and promoted through word-of-mouth or more formal mechanisms, such as publications and gatherings. The local environment should be taken into consideration in order to select the best method of communication for the particular organization (Shumaker and Makins, 2012). Finley (2013) suggests applying personal selling techniques, such as prospecting, cold calls, referrals, and up-selling, utilized by salespeople in the business world to gain traction as an embedded librarian. Embedded librarians typically offer additional value to their institutions through specialized research, technological, or instructional expertise (Shumaker, 2011). Despite the variations in embedded librarianship experiences, Shumaker and Makins (2012) assert, "the common threads are high competence, high customization, and high value" (p. 12). These successes must be evaluated and communicated, especially to those in managerial roles, in order to garner support for embedded librarian partnerships (Shumaker, 2011).

Administrative support can advance embedded librarian partnerships. Managers can encourage and enhance the success of embedded librarians by providing appropriate space, including librarians in group communications and collaborations, promoting librarian expertise among community members, and providing useful feedback (Shumaker, 2009). Due to the large amount of autonomy embedded librarians need to properly develop departmental relationships, managers must also trust that the librarians are utilizing their time effectively (Matos, Matsuoka-Motely, and Mayer, 2010, p. 132) While embedded librarian partnerships often begin as opportunities arise, ongoing commitments require strategic planning, especially in the area of curriculum development (Shumaker and Makins, 2012). Managers must allocate the necessary funding and resources to embedded services in order to maintain staffing cohesion and prevent librarians from suffering burnout (Shumaker, 2009).

LIBRARY INSTRUCTION AT THE MONROE LIBRARY, LOYOLA UNIVERSITY, NEW ORLEANS

Founded in 1912, Loyola is the largest Jesuit university in the southern United States. At its core, Jesuit education is founded on developing critical thinking skills along with the whole person, mind, body, and spirit. Social justice is a key element of Jesuit education, and the Loyola community strives to be men and women for and with others. Enrollment is approximately five thousand students including over three thousand undergraduates. Classes are small with a student-faculty ratio of 10:1. Five colleges on campus offer over sixty undergraduate degrees and over a dozen graduate and professional programs. Loyola uses Blackboard as its course management software. Faculty members maintain individual course pages either to supplement face-to-face courses or to facilitate online courses.

The Monroe Library serves as the primary library at Loyola. There are nearly a dozen members of the library faculty. Each librarian provides curricular expertise and services to enhance student learning. The librarian liaison program assigns a librarian to each area of study at the university. Librarian liaisons provide specialized outreach, collection development, and research and technology instruction for their liaison areas in order to further support the curriculum.

The instruction program at the Monroe Library is robust. Research and technology instruction includes teaching and co-teaching, embedded librarian experiences, one-shot library instruction sessions, individual appointments, reference assistance in the library's Learning Commons, and virtual chat and text services. In addition to the instructional work performed by librarian liaisons in their assigned areas, librarians also provide library instruction for other academic and student support services across campus and for schools and other community groups in the greater New Orleans area. Approximately two hundred fifty individual instruction sessions that reach over four thousand attendees are taught each year by the library faculty at the Monroe Library.

Library faculty members serve as the instructors of record for several courses. Research and Technology 2.0 is an eight-week, online, one-credit course taught by the library faculty, with the aim of teaching students to become more discerning and reflective information consumers and creators. The course covers critical issues, emerging technologies, and practical techniques that are relevant to the research process. Librarians have also co-taught the first-year seminar for students enrolled in Professional and Continuing Studies. The seminar, Thinking Critically, Acting Justly, was designed to be taught in the evening for nontraditional students. The course introduces students to a Jesuit education and issues related to social justice. Learning outcomes related to information literacy and the development of research and technological skills also play an important role in the seminar. Finally, Tech for Music is co-taught each fall by several librarians and members of the faculty from the College of Music and Fine Arts. Students rotate instructors as they progress through the course. Tech for Music is a requirement for students majoring in music, and exposes them to technologies for subject-specific research, musical composition, and self-promotion.

Library faculty members at the Monroe Library have increasingly become involved with their liaison areas and library instruction, and several librarians have participated in embedded librarian experiences. As the literature suggests, embedded librarianship assumes many definitions and applications across institutions. At the Monroe Library, embedded librarians are generally thought of as library faculty who are involved in the day-to-day activities of a course. These embedded librarianship experiences have involved co-teaching courses in a variety of disciplines.

CASE STUDIES

Historical Methods Lab

The instruction coordinator began her role as the librarian liaison to the Department of History in the fall semester of 2009. The History faculty had a tradition of being actively involved with the library in the area of collection development by primarily making requests for the purchase of materials. The area of library instruction, however, had yet to be developed. In addition to a master's in library science, the newly appointed librarian liaison to the Department of History also held a master's in history. She had acted as a teacher's assistant while working toward the degrees, which gave her practice in teaching about historical research. The librarian had previous experience from a position at another university in providing library instruction for history courses as a subject-area librarian. Her colleagues at Loyola were eager to introduce the new librarian liaison, who further reached out to the department through in-person meetings, e-mails, and a departmental meeting. She was able to introduce and promote library services, especially library instruction, through these interactions. Her collaborations with the Department of History grew over time, particularly with the course Historical Methods Lab.

Historical Methods Lab is the introductory course required of all students who major in history. The course introduces students to the basic skills that students need to further their coursework within the major. A few of the topics covered in the course are reading primary and secondary sources, performing historical research, creating citations, writing and editing drafts, and learning about scholarly ethics, such as practicing academic integrity and avoiding plagiarism. The content of the course is typically linked to the course US History to 1865, which covers American history to the Civil War. Students from outside of the major may enroll in US History to 1865, but it is a required course for History majors. Historical Methods Lab brings together all of the history majors who are enrolled across the multiple sections of US History to 1865 that are taught in the fall semester. While US History to 1865 is a regular three-credit course, Historical Methods Lab is a one-credit course that meets once a week for either fifty minutes or for one hour and fifteen minutes. Historical Methods Lab serves as a workshop for the research paper assigned in US History to 1865.

The librarian liaison's involvement with Historical Methods Lab evolved over several years. The faculty members in the Department of History rotate responsibility for the course each year. In the fall of 2009 and 2010, the librarian liaison provided overviews of library resources and services related to historical research. She communicated with the instructors and examined syllabi to identify what content was most pertinent to cover in the single class period. It was challenging to address all of the relevant material in a one-shot style of library instruction. By the fall of 2011, a second meeting with the librarian liaison was added to the Historical Methods Lab. A workshop later in the semester was created to allow students more time to work with the library resources introduced by the librarian. The librarian liaison and the instructor could then provide point-of-need guidance, because the students were fully immersed in their research projects. The faculty member from the Department of History scheduled to teach Historical Methods Lab in the fall of 2012 had worked multiple times with the librarian liaison to provide library instruction for several of his courses. After meeting to discuss their upcoming plans for Historical Methods Lab, the instructor and librarian liaison decided to move forward with an embedded librarian model.

The instructor and librarian liaison co-taught each class meeting of Historical Methods Lab. The instructor did express a concern that this collaboration might overburden the workload of the librarian, but the librarian's direct supervisor and colleagues were highly supportive. The instructor and librarian liaison began envisioning the course by revising the syllabus. The librarian liaison was incorporated into print materials and into the Blackboard course. They met before class each week to strategize and prepare for their time in the classroom. The instructor and librarian liaison co-lectured and jointly moderated discussion on the course topics, and other times planned for one of the instructors to take the instructional lead depending on the subject matter.

The introduction to the library and the follow-up workshop remained part of the course content, but the librarian liaison was now able to emphasize and reinforce research concepts throughout the course. Several topics were now approached in a different manner in the course. For example, citation managers were taught alongside a discussion and workshop on citation style. When both the instructor and the librarian liaison recognized that students struggled with reading historical monographs, they demonstrated how to strategically read a monograph, including techniques for effectively skimming the material. The students then learned from the librarian how to locate book reviews in library databases in order to identify contextual information by experts about monographs. In an introduction to using primary sources, the instructor related his experience working with archival materials for his research. The librarian then presented resources to the students that addressed questions and techniques for using primary resources in their research as a history major.

Both the instructor and the librarian liaison noted several benefits from their collaboration with Historical Methods Lab. The students appreciated having two points of view from the instructor and the librarian. The librarian liaison noticed that the history majors now recognized her more readily outside of class, and the students were more likely to approach her again for research advice. The librarian liaison became more involved with other faculty in the Department of History and related student activities. One of the great benefits of the embedded librarian experience was that a baseline of knowledge was established for all history majors that could be built upon in future coursework. A challenge still remained, however, in terms of how to further scaffold learning outcomes related to information literacy into the curriculum of the history major. Because the program of study is only partially sequential and courses are often open to students outside of the major, much of the same material must be readdressed in subsequent library instruction sessions. This reinforced exposure to research skills at the introductory level and again throughout the major is particularly helpful for students who elect to write a senior thesis. Overall, the instructor and the librarian liaison enjoyed the embedded librarian experience and have continued working collaboratively.

Interdisciplinary Humanities Research

In the spring semester of 2012, the librarian liaison to the University Honors Program (UHP) partnered with the director of the UHP to co-teach an interdisciplinary humanities research seminar for honors students. This partnership was the culmination of years of relationship-building between the library and the UHP.

In 2007 the dean of libraries called together a small group to develop a plan to enhance the library's relationship with the UHP. This small group created a plan that focused on enhanced student services, digitization of completed honors theses, expanded librarian involvement in the theses projects, and embedded reference. Working with a rotating cast of interim directors and codirectors of the UHP, this working group implemented extended borrowing privileges for library materials, policies and procedures for digitization of theses, an annual social gathering of librarians and thesis writers, and a short-lived and underutilized experience providing reference services a few hours per week in the honors lounge within the honors dormitory. Accomplishing this set of goals was challenging, as new relationships had to be established every time a new interim director was appointed.

In the fall of 2010, a permanent director was selected and an external review of the UHP was conducted. One of the recommendations of the external review was that the administrative office of the UHP be moved to a more central location for students. Eager to further collaborate with the UHP and to develop the learning commons model in the library, the library identified administrative and student space on the first floor of the library to bring the program within the library building. Although the new director of the UHP and the librarian liaison had already established a good rapport and had together institutionalized the digitization process for student theses, the co-location of their offices within the same building expanded their daily personal contact and opportunities for collaboration. Furthermore, the UHP director had enjoyed a close relationship, which included co-teaching, with a librarian at her prior institution, and had a personal interest in document collections and exhibits. These experiences led the librarian liaison and UHP director to investigate opportunities for co-teaching.

In 2011, many plans were underway at Loyola to celebrate the university's centennial in 2012. Knowing that centennial-related activities would be well received by the university community, the librarian liaison and UHP director agreed to focus an interdisciplinary humanities research seminar on the topic of centennials, bicentennials, and specifically the Loyola centennial. Together the pair identified and agreed on the following student learning outcomes for the course:

- Be able to understand and analyze the content and significance of a wide range of primary sources, including what kind of information they provide, biases, etc.
- Be able to conduct a thorough, productive search for secondary sources; understand the different types of secondary sources, what they are useful for, etc.
- Be able to use a variety of primary and secondary sources to create virtual and physical exhibits to a range of audiences
- Thoughtfully consider and analyze the goals and cultural roles of collections, archives, and exhibitions
- Understand the significance of centennial celebrations and participate therein
- Learn to use a variety of web-based tools to organize resources (e.g., RefWorks) and display findings (e.g., Camtasia)

- Create articulate, engaging, intellectually stimulating, and well-researched presentations
- Be prepared to serve as a research apprentice to faculty members in humanities disciplines
- Understand the importance of and draw critical connections among the events, foundings, and cultural currency of 1912
- Understand the business nature and monetary value of historic documents and artifacts

The course was limited in enrollment to current UHP students, but no other prerequisites were required. The resulting enrollment for the course included first-year students through seniors with majors from in a variety of disciplines.

The librarian liaison and the UHP director attended all classes and alternated between lecturing responsibility. Because the class met twice per week, the instructors often split duties by each lecturing once per week. On days when one of the instructors was not in charge of the lecturing, she was still engaged in the class discussion.

The introductory library assignment focused on students developing a shared understanding of 1912, becoming familiar with local and national newspaper sources, properly citing text and image resources, and demonstrating presentation best practices. In addition to demonstrations of News-Bank, the Louisiana Digital Library, and ProQuest Historical Newspapers, the librarian gave an overview of Prezi software, an online presentation editor. The librarian also modeled presentation best practices and a completed assignment through her presentation of "Libraries in 1912," a three-minute presentation, which included properly cited information and images from the resources that had been demonstrated. During the next two classes, students presented their three-minute 1912 in Context assignments on topics of their choice. The topics were diverse and represented the interdisciplinary nature of the course. The librarian used a rubric to grade the students' selection of sources, citation formatting, use of technology, and presentation skills.

Following the context assignment, students were engaged in discussions, presentations, and field experiences that revolved around primary documents and artifacts. Activities included a field trip to the Historic New Orleans Collection, a visit to the Monroe Library's Special Collections and Archives, and a lecture by a rare documents collector. During this time, students formed groups to focus on a digital exhibit project. In addition to the Loyola centennial project, students also had a choice of creating an exhibit for the centennial of the Louisiana Girl Scouts or the state of Louisiana's bicentennial. Once the students began focusing on their projects, the bulk of class time was used as demonstration and lab time. The librarian selected resources that were appropriate for each of the project groups, and the students worked independently within their groups to explore them.

The course coincided with a library initiative to bolster use of Special Collections and Archives materials, and the librarian facilitated the development of relationships with the faculty and staff in those areas. The group working on the Loyola centennial project acquired an unprocessed collection of historical documents from the Student Government Association and spent much of their lab time reviewing those documents, which they later donated to Special Collections and Archives. Other students in this group spent their lab time working with an archivist to locate university documents related to civil rights.

The course also provided two opportunities for experiential learning in the community. First, students were encouraged to opt-in for a service learning project at the local Girl Scouts headquarters. The librarian liaison and the UHP director worked with students to arrange and describe materials in the local Girl Scouts archive including uniforms, books, periodicals, and photographs. Because the students' digital exhibits had to coordinate with the prescheduled centennial and bicentennial celebrations that occurred several weeks before the end of the semester, another opportunity for experiential learning arose. The UHP director, who was also charged with developing collaborative scholarship on campus, and the librarian liaison decided to solve the problem by putting these now well-trained student researchers to work in the university community through a research apprenticeship project. Students provided the names of several faculty with whom they were interested in working, and the UHP director and librarian liaison made a letter of introduction. They provided a description of the types of research skills the students had acquired, a selection of appropriate projects that could be assigned to the students, and a grading rubric that the research mentors would need to complete if they chose to work with the students. Faculty embraced this opportunity for research support, and one student was selected by the university's president to work as a research apprentice.

The successes of the course were well publicized through institutional channels, including a university website feature ("Loyola University New Orleans Alumni Association," 2012), a university magazine (Schultheis, 2013), and the Provost's Annual Report ("Loyola University New Orleans," 2012). Additionally two students were invited to present posters on their group research projects at the 2012 National Collegiate Honors Council Annual Conference. The success of the course led to future plans for collaboration between the UHP director and librarian liaison, including an online research module to support thesis writers. The embedded experience also led to the development of closer relationships with students and the librarian liaison, the creation of faculty research mentors, and an opportunity for the librarian liaison to sit on the University Honors Advisory Board, to attend honors student social events, and to serve as the associate director of research, technology, and scholarship for the UHP.

Along with the positive outcomes of the embedded experience, the co-instructors identified some areas for improvement. These include:

- Clarify each instructor's roles to identify who will lead which classes and who will grade each assignment.
- Determine the need for course prerequisites to address difficulties with varying research skill levels.
- Reduce the number of group projects topics to allow deeper, more focused demonstration and exploration of library resources.
- Ensure that completed sample projects are available to students.
- Create an online system to collect grading rubrics from research apprentice mentors.

Overall the experience was a valuable one that furthered the collaboration between not just the librarian liaison and the UHP director, but also between multiple library professionals and the students enrolled in the course.

Introduction to Music Industry Studies

The Department of Music Industry Studies (MIS) at Loyola prepares students for careers in music law, marketing, management, administration, and multimedia production, among others. Shortly after Loyola reopened in 2006 after a semester-long hiatus due to Hurricane Katrina, the head of the MIS Department expressed interest in involving a librarian with the program's introductory class, because he found that the students were unfamiliar with basic research and technology skills. The students were relying heavily on unreliable sources, and they were both intentionally and unintentionally plagiarizing their work, as many of them did not understand that they had to credit information freely available on the Internet (Willey, 2013). A librarian began working with the class primarily on research and citation skills and the basics of using Microsoft Office. From that time until 2011, a variety of librarians worked with the course and gradually redesigned it to be more student centered. The course's final project involved a research paper and a PowerPoint presentation, and 20 percent of their final grade and research paper grade came from work graded by the librarian.

In 2011, a newly hired librarian with master's degrees in both music and library science became the librarian liaison to the MIS program. Her involvement with the course coincided with the MIS department's complete redesign of the course material and final project. Continual assessment of the success of the course has also led to additional changes since 2011.

The class meets with MIS faculty Mondays, Wednesdays, and every other Friday, and the librarian meets with the class on the Fridays in between. The course provides students with an overview of the music industry, and with it a chance to try different career paths including management, creative services, artists and repertoire, marketing, legal, and finance. The students are put into production companies of five to six members, where each student takes on one of these roles in order to promote a band or artist. As their final project, the group must produce an extended play (EP) recording, a concert or a video; set up a website for their artist; and write detailed business plans for each deliverable. The business plans must exhibit research, and this counts for 20 percent of their final project grade.

When the class meets with the librarian liaison, they work on developing skills that will aid them in their production deliverables and business plans. These include evaluating information sources, using the library's resources for research, avoiding plagiarism, citing using MLA, creating a professional web presence including a website and social media, and using spreadsheet software to create budgets and graphs. Individual assignments for the librarian also account for 20 percent of the students' final grades. The librarian liaison coordinates and teaches most of the librarian-led classes, but also works with other librarians either on individual class periods or, when more than one section of the class is being taught, by co-teaching or splitting the sections with one or more librarians.

A few tools facilitate this embedded experience. The MIS faculty member and the embedded librarian share a course page in Blackboard. Assignments for the librarian, including the research portion of the final project, utilize grading rubrics. There is also a course-specific research guide which details the best library resources for the different jobs the students hold in their groups.

Over time, the course has relied less on teaching technology skills and more on active learning. Online tutorials of library databases are linked in Blackboard, so that students can familiarize themselves with the databases before class and spend more hands-on time in class, similar to a flipped classroom. The redesigned final project involving the student production companies is more indicative of the course's learning outcomes than the research paper, which was assigned previously and allows the students to immerse themselves in the music industry. The production groups have to present their deliverables to the class and a panel of MIS faculty members; the librarian works with the students on presentation best practices rather than teaching specific presentation software. In addition, requests from faculty that the students know how to "define their audience" led to the teaching of social media best practices. The only specific software that is taught stems from requests from MIS faculty for website development (WordPress) and spreadsheet creation and data analysis (Excel and Google Sheets).

There are also challenges to this approach that have informed modifications to the course over time. As is repeated throughout the literature on embedded librarianship, the workload can be intense, and effective time management as well as the support of library administration is a necessity. But the biggest challenge to this particular course relates to its fragmented nature, since students meet either with MIS faculty or a librarian liaison but never together. Class content between the Monday/Wednesday MIS faculty and the Friday librarian are supposed to reflect each other, but that is not always successful. Initially the librarian liaison met with the class every Friday for the first ten weeks of the semester. Both student grades and student evaluation forms reflected that this approach led to students forgetting their research skills by the time the final project was actually due. This has improved with the every-other-week library schedule, but students are now sometimes confused about when they are meeting with the librarian and when they are meeting with the MIS faculty. There is also general confusion from students about who is teaching what—questions about the librarian liaison's assignments frequently go to the MIS faculty and vice-versa. Student feedback is collected at the end of each semester to inform future planning and, while the feedback is generally very positive, the biggest complaint from students is that they do not see how the research classes tie into their final project. This shows that better integration of library research and technology into the bigger picture of the course is necessary.

Still, the advantages to embedding a librarian in this course are evident. As soon as the library became involved in this class, the MIS department head found that the students' research and technology skills improved. Since this is an introductory course, librarians are predominantly introducing students to library research their first semester of college. Because of the breadth of the library's involvement with this class, reference librarians are clued in to what assignments the students will be asking for help with. The librarians who work with the course have the opportunity to inform and aid teaching faculty in developing alternative research assignments, and the embedded librarians get the experience of developing and assessing assignments. Because of the long-standing relationship between the library and MIS, support for the course has been cultivated by the library administration, as they can see that the librarians, teaching faculty, and students all benefit from enhanced engagement within this course.

Synoptic Gospels

In spring semester of 2011 a professor in the Department of Religious Studies and the librarian liaison to the Department of Religious Studies partnered for an embedded librarian experience in the course The Synoptic Gospels.

The groundwork for the embedded librarian experience started with a new librarian liaison appointment to the Department of Religious Studies in the fall semester of 2009. During his first semester at the Monroe Library, the librarian undertook instruction opportunities as they arose. When a research instruction request came from a newly hired professor to teach her classes how to find commentaries and biblical criticism, the librarian agreed to teach the request despite having no prior experience with biblical research. After two successful instruction sessions, the librarian was assigned as the librarian liaison to the Department of Religious Studies.

During the next two semesters, the professor and librarian liaison worked together on a number of classes, predominantly standard research instruction sessions. Each one was geared toward the specific needs of the course, and all of the courses involved some form of information literacy instruction. One notable experience that paved the way for a fully embedded experience was a collaboration with the professor during her first year seminar in fall of 2010. For this course the librarian liaison became a frequent visitor and instructed students on a number of topics, including using blogs, plagiarism prevention, and library research.

Despite the established relationship between the professor and librarian, the idea for an embedded experience came about by chance circumstance. The librarian liaison and the professor met in the fall of 2010 to discuss library support for a study abroad program in Rome. As this conversation expanded, it became clear that there was a lot to gain from a more immediate collaboration. At this point, the librarian proposed taking on the role of an embedded librarian in an upcoming course the professor was teaching. This role was designed to serve two purposes. First, it would expand the librarian's subject knowledge in biblical studies, providing immediate benefit to his liaison area. Second, this experience would allow for the immediate inclusion of library instruction during the day-to-day aspects of the course.

The Synoptic Gospels is an upper-level course. It is primarily designed for religious studies majors and minors, although students can choose to take the course as an elective if they meet the prerequisite requirements. The course itself is a critical exploration of the books of Matthew, Mark, and Luke from the Christian Bible.

Preparation for the course began immediately. The "eureka" moment for full librarian integration came during the preparation of supplementary material for the course. Using the screen-capture software Camtasia, the librarian and professor were recording a tutorial on how to use the book *A Synopsis of the Four Gospels* published by the American Bible Society. This tutorial sparked the idea that students could use the software to produce video essays as an assignment for the course. It was the librarian liaison's duty to oversee the technical instruction and troubleshooting for the students' progress on this project. The spring 2011 course was run as a seminar-style course taught in the library. Twelve religious studies majors or minors at various points in their academic careers enrolled in the course. The students were evaluated on class participation, two discussion-based tests, a group video presentation, and a final paper. During the course, the librarian read all of the class texts and was a full participant in course discussions.

The librarian provided two information literacy instruction sessions for the course. The first was a tour of the library early on in the course. Students were shown where the books on Matthew, Mark, and Luke were located in the stacks and where the Bible commentaries were located in the library's reference section. This was particularly important for the integrated research aspects of the course. The professor and librarian attempted to have students use the materials at their disposal to answer questions rather than simply give them the answers. The class also received instruction focused on using databases to find Biblical criticism for the students' video presentations and final papers.

The video presentations, officially called the Camtasia Projects, were one of the most inspiring elements of the course. For these projects, students were split into four groups of three students and assigned to create a critical video essay using Camtasia. After showing the video in class, the students were required to lead a class discussion on the video. Groups were assigned to pick one verse from the book of Mark or Matthew. After a brief meeting with the librarian to discuss the software, groups worked on their own to complete the project. The requirements for the video essays were minimal. The students were required to visually interpret their critical exegesis through videos of less than five minutes. These projects were a resounding success. The videos showed high-quality production and research. Because students came to class with the presentation fully prepared, the presentations stayed on schedule. The videos also paved the way for the students to apply the research skills they used in the creation of the presentation for their final papers on a verse from the Book of Luke (Sullivan, 2013).

Overall, this experience was deemed a success by the parties involved. While it did take the librarian liaison away from other duties, such as reference desk shifts, the librarian's colleagues were supportive of this endeavor. The embedded experience had numerous benefits for the librarian liaison, professor, and course. First, the librarian's knowledge of biblical studies increased exponentially. The language of the discipline, key texts, and critical methods learned throughout this course have affected everything from collection development to the librarian liaison's work with other liaison departments. The course benefitted from having an intermediary between the professor and the students—as one student aptly described during a professional development presentation on embedded librarianship, "[the librarian] was more than a student, but not the professor." This interstitial role that the librarian liaison occupied allowed a safe space for students to interact both inside of and outside of class. Because the librarian liaison was not in charge of assigning grades, he was able to encourage lively debate on numerous topics. Outside of class, students approached the librarian liaison for content editing on their final papers. The professor benefitted from the librarian liaison's presence through the Camtasia projects. Having the technological weight of the project off of the professor's shoulders let her concentrate on the course content, while the librarian liaison concentrated on the technical aspects of the project.

CONCLUSION

As described in this chapter, there is substantial professional literature surrounding embedded librarianship. While the precise definition of an embedded librarian varies throughout the scholarly canon, the common theme of librarians connecting with their users by meeting them in their own environment clearly emerges throughout the scholarship.

The case studies in this chapter highlight the opportunities as well as the continuing challenges associated with embedded experiences. While embedding in courses creates a rewarding experience for students, faculty, and librarians alike, the necessary time commitment from the librarian requires careful planning and support from administration. In environments such as those at Loyola's Monroe Library, the time commitment has been not only prioritized by individual librarians, but also valued on an institutional level. Such an environment is necessary to capitalize on the documented outcomes of rich embedded librarian activities. Through reading the embedded librarian experiences described at Loyola, other librarians and instructors may develop ideas for deepened library and student engagement at their institutions.

REFERENCES

Bell, Steven. 2013. "Preface." In *Embedded Librarianship: What Every Academic Librarian Should Know*, vii–i. Santa Barbara, CA: Libraries Unlimited.
Brower, Cassandra. 2011. "A Recent History of Embedded Librarianship: Collaboration and Partnership Building with Academics in Learning and Research Environments." In *Embedded Librarians: Moving beyond One-Shot Instruction*, 3–16. Chicago: Association of College and Research Libraries.
Dewey, Barbara I. 2004. "The Embedded Librarian: Strategic Campus Collaborations." *Resource Sharing & Information Networks* 17 (1/2): 5–17. doi: 10.1300/J121v17n01_02.:10.1300/J121v17n01_02.
Doerksen, Brad. 2013. "A Different Kind of Embedded Librarian: More Than Just a New Office." *Christian Librarian* 56 (2): 80–82.
Drewes, Kathy, and Nadine Hoffman. 2010. "Academic Embedded Librarianship: An Introduction." *Public Services Quarterly* 6 (2): 75–82. doi: 10.1080/15228959.2010.498773.
Federer, Lisa. 2013a. "Embedded with the Scientists: The UCLA Experience." *Journal of eScience Librarianship* 2 (1): 6. http://dx.doi.org/10.7191/jeslib.2013.1039.

———. 2013b. "The Librarian as Research Informationist: A Case Study." *Journal of the Medical Library Association* 101 (4): 298. doi: 10.3163/1536-5050.101.4.011.

Finley, Wayne E. 2013. "Using Personal Selling Techniques in Embedded Librarianship." *Journal of Business & Finance Librarianship* 18 (4): 279–92. doi: 10.1080/08963568.2013.825111.

Guillot, Ladonna, Beth Stahr, and Bonnie J. Meeker. 2010. "Nursing Faculty Collaborate with Embedded Librarians to Serve Online Graduate Students in a Consortium Setting." *Journal of Library & Information Services in Distance Learning* 4 (1/2): 53–62. doi: 10.1080/15332901003666951.

Hamilton, Buffy J. 2012. "Case Profile: Ellen Hampton Filgo." *Library Technology Reports* 48 (2): 16–20. doi: 10.5860/ltr.

Hawes, Sandra Lee. 2011. "Playing to Win: Embedded Librarians in Online Classrooms." *Journal of Library & Information Services in Distance Learning* 5 (1/2): 56–66. doi: 10.1080/1533290X.2011.570560.

Heider, Kelly L. 2010. "Ten Tips for Implementing a Successful Embedded Librarian Program." *Public Services Quarterly* 6 (2/3): 110–21. doi: 10.1080/15228959.2010.498765.

Helms, Marilyn M., and Melissa Whitesell. 2013. "Transitioning to the Embedded Librarian Model and Improving the Senior Capstone Business Strategy Course." *Journal of Academic Librarianship* 39 (September): 401–13. doi: 10.1016/j.acalib.2013.03.015.

Hines, Samantha. 2013. "A Brief History of Embedded Librarianship." In *Embedded Librarianship: What Every Academic Librarian Should Know*, 1–12. Santa Barbara, CA: Libraries Unlimited.

Kelly, Rob. 2008. "Team Teaching with an Embedded Librarian." *Online Classroom*, October, 7–8.

Kenefick, Colleen. 2011. "The Case for Embedded Hospital Librarianship." *Journal of Hospital Librarianship* 11 (2): 195–99. doi: 10.1080/15323269.2011.558407.

Knight, Valerie R., and Charissa Loftis. 2012. "Moving from Introverted to Extraverted Embedded Librarian Services: An Example of a Proactive Model." *Journal of Library & Information Services in Distance Learning* 6 (3/4): 362–75. doi: 10.1080/1533290X.2012.705165.

Li, Judy. 2012. "Serving as an Educator: A Southern Case in Embedded Librarianship." *Journal of Business & Finance Librarianship* 17 (2): 133–52. doi: 10.1080/08963568.2012.661198.

Long, Dallas. 2011. "Embedded Right Where the Students Live: A Librarian in the University Residence Halls." In *Embedded Librarians: Moving beyond One-Shot Instruction*, 199–210. Chicago: Association of College and Research Libraries.

Loyola University New Orleans. 2012. "Loyola University New Orleans Provost's Report." *Issuu*. http://issuu.com/loyola-university-new-orleans/docs/luno__12_provost_report.

Loyola University New Orleans Alumni Association. 2012. "Girl Scouts Join Loyola in Centennial Celebration." March 9, http://alumni.loyno.edu/pack-press/girl-scouts-join-loyola-centennial-celebration.

Martin, Elaine R. 2013. "Shaping Opportunities for the New Health Sciences Librarian." *Journal of the Medical Library Association* 101 (4): 252–53. doi: 10.3163/1536.

Matos, Michael A., Nobue Matsuoka-Motley, and William Mayer. 2010. "The Embedded Librarian Online or Face-to-Face: American University's Experiences." *Public Services Quarterly* 6 (2/3): 130–39. doi: 10.1080/15228959.2010.497907.

McCluskey, Clare. 2013. "Being an Embedded Research Librarian: Supporting Research by Being a Researcher." *Journal of Information Literacy* 7 (2): 4–14. http://dx.doi.org/10.11645/7.2.1815.

Mon, Lorri, and Lydia Eato Harris. 2011. "The Death of the Anonymous Librarian." *The Reference Librarian* 52 (4): 352–64. doi: 10.1080/02763877.2011.585279.

Schulte, Stephanie J. 2012. "Embedded Academic Librarianship: A Review of the Literature." *Evidence Based Library & Information Practice* 7 (4): 122–38.

Schultheis, Shelby. 2013. "Exceptional Experiences for Exceptional Students." *Loyola University New Orleans Magazine*. http://magazine.loyno.edu/exceptional-experiences-exceptional-students.

Shumaker, David. 2009. "Who Let the Librarians Out?" *Reference & User Services Quarterly* 48 (3): 239–42. http://www.jstor.org/stable/20865079.
———. 2011. "Succeeding with Embedded Librarianship." *Information Outlook* 15 (4): 30–32.
———. 2012a. "Embedded Librarians in Special Libraries." *Information Today* 29 (7): 1–34.
———. 2012b. "The Embedded Librarians." *Online* 36 (4): 24–27.
Shumaker, David, and Alison Makins. 2012. "Lessons from Successful Embedded Librarians." *Information Outlook* 16 (3): 10–12.
Shumaker, David, and Mary Talley. 2009. *Models of Embedded Librarianship: Final Report.* Alexandria, VA: Special Libraries Association. http://hq.sla.org/pdfs/EmbeddedLibrarian-shipFinalRptRev.pdf.
———. 2010. "Models of Embedded Librarian: A Research Summary." *Information Outlook* 14 (1): 26–35.
Sullivan, Brian. 2013. "Developing 21st Century Learning Outcomes through Student-Created Videos." *Ubiquitous Learning: An International Journal* 5 (1): 49–55.
Talley, Mary. 2011. "Success and the Embedded Librarian." *Information Outlook* 15 (3): 25–28. https://www.sla.org/wp-content/uploads/2013/05/Success_and_the_Embedded.pdf.
Tumbleson, Beth E., and John J. Burke. 2010. "Embedded Librarianship Is Job One: Building on Instructional Synergies." *Public Services Quarterly* 6 (2): 225–36. doi: 10.1080/15228959.2010.497457.
Willey, Malia. 2013. "Amplify the Active Learning: Revamping Course-Integrated Library Instruction to Be Student Centered." *LOEX Conference Proceedings 2011*, December 2013, http://commons.emich.edu/loexconf2011/22.
Wu, Lin, Virginia Trotter Betts, Susan Jacob, Richard Nollan, and Tommie Norris. 2013. "Making Meaningful Connections: Evaluating an Embedded Librarian Pilot Project to Improve Nursing Scholarly Writing." *Journal of the Medical Library Association* 101 (4): 323–26. doi: 10.3163/1536-5050.101.4.016
York, Amy C., and Jason M. Vance. 2009. "Taking Library Instruction into the Online Classroom: Best Practices for Embedded Librarians." *Journal of Library Administration* 49 (1/2): 197–209. doi: 10.1080/01930820802312995.

Chapter Ten

Democratizing Digital

The Highway 89 Digital Collection and the Promise of Inclusive Online Collaboration

Brad Cole, Clint Pumphrey, and Liz Woolcott

Highway 89 Digital Collections (www.highway89.org) is a collaborative digital exhibit initiated by the Utah Manuscript Association (UMA) to document the development of twentieth-century Utah and the Intermountain West through the story of U.S. Highway 89.[1] The project grew out of UMA's desire to work together on a meaningful collaborative digital project that accomplishes the following: collects digital content that is useful to researchers and the general public, creates a simple process for cultural entities or individuals to upload digital content to the site without an intermediary, allows for user comments, and scales to accommodate material from other states. The result is a digital exhibit with an attractive display and a simple interface for both users and contributors. A work in progress, Highway 89 Digital Collections continues to add new members from the Utah cultural community and reach out to similar institutions in Arizona, Idaho, Wyoming, and Montana.

An important catalyst for the final decision to feature U.S. Highway 89 was a presentation about Route 66 by archivists from the Society of Southwest Archivists (SSA) and the National Park Service given at a joint conference for SSA and the Conference of American Archivists in Mesa, Arizona, in May 2012 (Barthuli, Day, and Evans, 2012). This panel discussed their efforts to create a web presence for the storied Route 66, demonstrating the interest and excitement in highway history and explaining the myriad of historical and cultural topics that could be supported by chronicling the history of a highway. Like Route 66, U.S. Highway 89 is important to the devel-

**Figure 10.1. Hi-Way 89 Lodge road sign in Garfield County, Utah. Utah State
Archives and Records Service, Outdoor Advertising Sign Inventories, Series 959,
Box 3. Folder 15.** *Used by permission, Utah State Archives, all rights reserved*

opment of the West in the twentieth century, a period of history that has not
been as well-documented in archives and on digital websites as nineteenth-
century history. These factors solidified the idea of using U.S. Highway 89 as
a conduit to create a meaningful digital collaborative.

U.S. Highway 89 traverses Utah and the Intermountain West from north
to south, passing through many of the region's points of natural splendor,
while at the same time tying together many of its major population areas and
cultures.

Prior to the decommissioning of the southernmost section in 1992, one
could begin driving on the highway at Nogales, Arizona, a small community
on the Mexican border. During the trip, the intrepid traveler would pass
through southwest Arizona, the color country of southern Utah, and the
mountainous regions of the Wasatch range, clipping a piece of Idaho at Bear
Lake before continuing to the twin national park treasures of Grand Teton
and Yellowstone National Parks. The final leg would take the traveler north
through Montana, intersecting the Going to the Sun Highway in Glacier
National Park before ending up at Piegan, Montana, on the Canadian border.

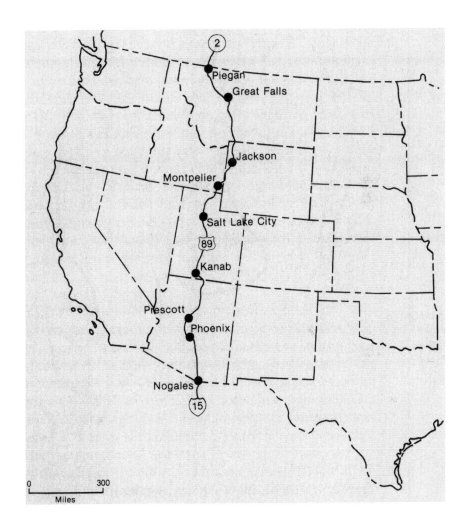

Figure 10.2. Map of U.S. Highway 89. *From Western Images, Western Landscapes: Travels Along U.S. 89, by Thomas R. Vale and Geraldine R. Vale. © 1990 The Arizona Board of Regents. Reprinted by permission of the University of Arizona Press*

In fact, a total of seven national parks—Saguaro, Grand Canyon, Zion, Bryce, Grand Teton National Park, Yellowstone National Park, and Glacier—line the road, as well as numerous national monuments. Towns and cities along the route such as Tucson, Phoenix, and Salt Lake City, which were small commercial centers when Highway 89 was established in the late 1920s, are now the corridor's booming metropolitan areas. The road also encounters numerous Native American tribes, from southern Arizona's Tohono O'dham (formerly Papago), Pima, Yavapai, and Apache and northern Arizona's Navajo and Hopi tribes, to the Paiute and Ute lands of southern and central Utah and the Shoshone and Bannock Country of northern Utah, before finally venturing into the Blackfoot and Flathead regions of Montana.

From an historical perspective, the history of U.S. Highway 89 chronicles the transformation of a large swath of the Southwest and the Intermountain West during the twentieth century. From an archival point of view, the hidden treasures to be gleaned and shared with researchers and the public are numerous and varied. The long-term potential for partnerships with large research institutions, small historical societies, museums, and Native American archives, to name just a few, are enticing.

Collaborative digital projects, where multiple repositories contribute content, have become fairly ubiquitous for several years. Up to this point there have been three fairly common models. One model, like that of the Mountain West Digital Library (MWDL, http://mwdl.org/), aggregates material from several institutions within a region and hosts the material on a website. These type of aggregated collections function like a digital special collections repository in that they host a large variety of topics and content. Researchers work through the material as they would in a special collections reading room. They are rich sites for researchers to explore primary sources. These sites, unlike the Highway 89 Digital Collection website, often have a more complex infrastructure as well as a more complex method for uploading content.

Aggregating content based on a specific topic is another common collaborative model. A good example of this is the Western Waters Digital Library (http://westernwaters.org/). This online collection, the brainchild of the Greater Western Library Association (GWLA), originally documented collections related to four major western river basins (the Colorado, Columbia, Platte, and Rio Grande) and later expanded to cover water across the entire West. The Western Waters Digital Library utilizes a harvesting platform that aggregates thematic content from specific collections at contributing institutions. Both the Western Waters Digital Library and the Mountain West Digital Library are a boon for researchers; however, both tend to be more sophisticated, employing a complex infrastructure that relies heavily on trained professionals to curate, catalog, manage, and harvest content. This high-end approach works well for large institutions, but it can be difficult for institutions with limited means or personnel to replicate or contribute content.

A third model, used by the National Park Service in developing the National Park Service Route 66 Corridor Preservation Program website (http://ncptt.nps.gov/rt66/), is basically a clearinghouse of information about a topic, but with little digital content of its own. Of interest to the Highway 89 project is the Route 66 Archives Research Collaborative (ARC) website, a subsite of the larger park service site that offers a portal to ten different institutions that tout Route 66 museums or collections. The page explores the historic relevance and context of Route 66 and explains the process of researching with primary source materials.

Recently, libraries have become more proactive in their approach to collecting digital content. They schedule scanning events at public entities, such as libraries or museums, and invite the public to bring historical documents and photographs to be digitized and added to online collections. In 2010 Utah State University (USU) set up a scanning event along these lines at the Elko, Nevada, Cowboy Poetry Gathering. Though the event proved time-consuming and was not able to accommodate a large number of participants, it successfully captured content that is now part of the Ranch Family Documentation Project (http://digital.lib.usu.edu/cdm/landingpage/collection/ranchoral). More ambitious is the Pioneers in Your Attic (http://mwdl.org/portals/pioneers.php) project in Utah, sponsored by the MWDL, which is having good success although still in its infancy. Larger-scale projects such as the Civil War in Your Attic digital collection project in Maryland (http://collections.digitalmaryland.org/cdm/landingpage/collection/mcw) have resulted in an immense amount of new content being captured. The proactive approach to digitizing privately held historical material demonstrated by these projects has been a constructive way to involve the public in building collaborative archives. These types of collections, while highly successful, are still fairly labor intensive, requiring a great deal of planning while limiting the number of participants due to location and scheduling. There can also be quite a bit of lead time between scanning the material and actually loading the items onto a website.

Spurred on by the work of the Route 66 consortium and these other collaborative digital projects, the UMA created a subgroup to begin work on the Highway 89 Digital Collection. The Highway 89 project partners set out to create a website that would explore an under-documented topic—Highway 89 and twentieth-century Western development—and create a simplified, intuitive interface that would allow smaller institutions and individuals the opportunity to easily add content. The initial group consisted of six members of the UMA—Utah State University, Utah State Archives, Salt Lake County Archives, Brigham Young University, and Southern Utah University, as well as one out-of-state partner, Northern Arizona University.

Fortunately for the group, the state of Utah was chosen to participate in the ILEAD: Innovative Librarians Explore, Apply, and Discover (https://ileadusa.wordpress.com/) program, which started in Illinois in 2010 and expanded to five other states in 2013. ILEAD funding came from an IMLS grant and asked for proposals that established teams to "create a resource that will meet the needs of your collective communities." This seemed to fit the project perfectly and a subset of the UMA committee, consisting of three representatives from USU, one from Southern Utah University, and one from the Utah State Archives, was successfully selected as one of eight teams. This provided the catalyst to get the Highway 89 project off and running.

The UMA committee and its ILEAD representatives had three main goals in creating a Highway 89 website. First, create a user-friendly site that would allow for all cultural institutions, regardless of size or capability, to easily add content to the site without the help of an intermediary. Second, make the site scalable to allow for content contribution not only from other Utah institutions, but also from institutions within the four other states that U.S. Highway 89 traverses. Finally, build an interface that would be simple for the public to navigate and add content.

Creating long-term, sustainable, online collaborations involving partners that vary in both size and resource capacity presented somewhat of a challenge. Stakeholders, running the gamut from the contributors supplying the content to the consumers who ultimately utilize the content, presented conflicting demands that had to be resolved. Not least among these challenges was keeping usability in mind while trying to simplify the content creation process for partners. The intersection between simplification for users and simplification for partners was an important balance to achieve.

Early discussion about the content of the Highway 89 Digital Collections website included the potential for developing a web page that acted as a bibliography or directory of content, much like the Route 66 ARC. As the most simplistic and easily accomplished method of gathering content, contributing partners with existing web presences felt an initial pull in this direction to minimize any duplication of their efforts. This would essentially entail a long list of links to current collections and resources. This had two drawbacks, however: not all partners in the collaborative had web presences to link to, and 1995 web standards had died an ignominious death long ago. Exploration of sites that acted as digital bibliographies provided a very real understanding of the frustration users experience in coming across lists of links that are difficult to evaluate, given their limited experience with the unfamiliar websites and understandably limited knowledge of their scope of the content. A "one-stop shop" that directly housed images, text, and audio from all contributors, regardless of whether it appeared elsewhere on the Web, was considered the best experience from the perspective of the user. It also allowed partners without websites or databases to upload their material and have a presence on the Web. An additional bonus to this setup was the possibility of developing further collaboration with material, such as building joint exhibits.

The collaborative partners evaluated several digital asset management systems (DAMS) for creating the Highway 89 Digital Collections website, including CONTENTdm, Omeka, and Drupal. Issues affecting contributing partners ranged from accessibility and cost, to learning curves for uploading and manipulating content, to the potential for contributing content to larger digital collaboratives such as the Mountain West Digital Library (MWDL) and the Digital Public Library of America (DPLA). One special consideration was the ability to create visually appealing and intuitive interfaces to help invite patron use of material and present the story of Highway 89 in narrative formats that traditional DAMS do not provide.

Testing and review of the DAMS revealed a great deal of potential for the Omeka platform, which combined the digital asset management benefits of CONTENTdm and the visual interfaces of a Drupal site. In particular, its most appealing quality was its flexibility. Partners without existing websites or DAMS could upload and control their own content with no other specialized software than an Internet browser and a spreadsheet. Partners who had content already in a DAMS could pull their material into Omeka via an OAI harvest instead of manually uploading it, thereby helping to eliminate some of the duplication of effort. In addition to its OAI harvesting capabilities, Omeka could also act as an OAI repository, allowing other aggregators like MWDL to pull content from it. This was especially appealing to partners who lacked an on-ramp into MWDL's collaborative.

First and foremost, however, Omeka gave the Highway 89 Digital Collections website the ability to provide engaging visual interfaces to patrons through maps, timelines, and exhibits. Traditionally, patrons use search terms that lead them to a set of items displayed in a list. With Omeka, collection material could be pinned on a map at the location from which it originated or it described, giving patrons the ability to see how content related to one another through location. Just as maps pinned with the location of the digital item would show geographic overlap, timelines depicting dates of events or creation of items demonstrate time periods when activity took place along Highway 89. Digital objects can also be contextualized through the development of exhibits that explore themes within the Highway 89 Digital Collections content, such as architecture or advertising.

One truly exciting possibility offered by the Omeka platform was the ability to allow the public to upload their own content to the website. This allowed Highway 89 Digital Collections to accept images, audio, video, or text to the website from individuals in addition to those from formal institutions such as archives, museums, or libraries. By providing a whole new level of service when it comes to archiving and telling the story of Highway 89, the history of Highway 89 would not be told just through officially archived sources, but through the contributed memories of individuals who had experienced it.

The collaborative partners felt that the visual interfaces and contributor tools offered by Omeka were crucial to the user experience. The ability to implement them was not readily available in most of the DAMS reviewed. Workarounds for providing these interfaces on top of other DAMS would involve a significant amount of time on the part of the technical team, and were therefore not considered a good long-term investment.

The technicalities of implementing an Omeka system, on the other hand, were fairly minimal. Out of the box, Omeka comes with a very minimalist website layout and specific functions, mostly centered on uploading content. For Omeka users who are hosting their own version of Omeka, however, all of the additional plugins that have been developed are available for free. These plugins include items such as an exhibit builder function, Google Maps for providing the map-based interface, OAI harvesting and repository features, timelines, and YouTube and Sound Cloud integration. One systems administrator was able to download the open source solution onto a local server and add the plugins necessary to operate the website as desired with little effort.

Of the initial collaborative partners, USU volunteered to host the website and content and take on the responsibility for setup, maintenance, security, and long-term sustainability. As mentioned above, this required the part-time commitment of a systems administrator. The initial installation required about two to four hours of time, and required familiarity with server setup and application installation processes. Developing the website layout was a bit more intensive, requiring about 10 percent of the system administrator's time, with the majority of that effort expended in the first four to five weeks learning how to code for responsive web design formats.

Several of the features requested by the initial collaborative partners were not available in plugin formats at the time and had to be coded by hand. Now, almost two years later, most of those features are available as plugins. Additional costs included the server and the server maintenance, which were also assumed by USU. Estimated costs of the server and ongoing maintenance average about $750 per year.

In addition to the systems administrator, implementation of the website required a metadata librarian to establish standard guidelines and rules for content ingestion. The result was the Highway 89 Metadata and Submission Guidelines, which delineated the metadata fields that were required for each item submitted to the repository, as well as standards for the digital files themselves. The guidelines included step-by-step instructions on how to use Omeka to upload content in three different processes—individually, in batches, and via an OAI harvest—in an effort to accommodate the different styles that contributing institutions would need.

The submission guidelines were built on the Mountain West Digital Library metadata application profile, which the majority of the collaborative partners were already familiar with. For simplicity's sake, it used Dublin Core as the metadata format, though some requirements for fields like Coverage-Spatial (dcterms:spatial) were modified to encourage partners to include information necessary to build the visual interfaces for the maps.

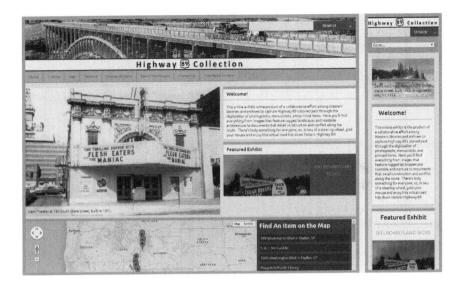

Figure 10.3. Side-by-side comparison of the desktop and mobile versions of Highway 89 Digital Collections' website

Since the process for contributing content to the website was focused on simplicity, very little training was needed. Collaborative partners were basically given the Metadata and Submission Guidelines, as well as unique logins to the website, and left to their own discretion to decide what and how much to contribute at their own pace. All found this process to be simple and were able to integrate it into their workflows. One partner commented that the Submission Guidelines were "easy to follow" and also found that the use of the supplied metadata template spreadsheet made the process of uploading in batches "infinitely easier" (K. Krattley, personal communication, February 27, 2015).

Early on in the discussion about DAMS, the collaborative partners agreed that each institution should be responsible for submitting their own content instead of sending it to the hosting partner for uploading. This would help reduce the burden on the host partner and avoid bottlenecks as content was uploaded. Developing a workflow that allowed each partner the ability to not only upload their own content on their own time schedule, but also edit and take down their material as needed, was seen as an essential step toward long-term sustainability. There was a modest amount of success in this formula. Some of the partnering institutions were quick to put up their material and have maintained a fairly steady pace of contributions. Other institutions found that they could not contribute at a regular pace and have had times where their content contribution has been sporadic and slow. This was to be

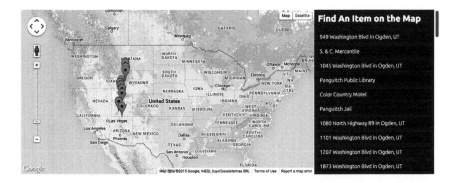

Figure 10.4.   The Google Map plugin in Omeka identifies collection items in a simple visual interface

expected, but does present a challenge for keeping a steady flow of new material.

Many of challenges and successes of the Highway 89 project can be examined through the participation of three institutions: the Salt Lake County Archives, Southern Utah University Special Collections, and the Brigham City Museum. The enthusiastic involvement of these smaller archives and museums has indicated a demand for such collaborative exhibits, and has provided the project organizers with some useful test cases to assist and encourage potential participants in the future.

Despite a staff of just one full-time employee and a part-time employee, the Salt Lake County Archives (http://admin.slco.org/archives/) agreed to be an early contributor to the Highway 89 project, and at this point has digitized and uploaded 208 items—the third most of any contributor. The archive's current web presence is largely a research guide, which provides links to information and finding aids that pertain to property and house history, county government history, and family history. What digital content they do have is limited to birth and death records and some online exhibits, although additional functionality is in the works. Like many smaller institutions, their biggest obstacle to digital content creation is a lack of funding to hire additional staff.

The Highway 89 exhibit, therefore, provided the county archives staff with the opportunity to jumpstart their online content, largely with photographs from their property tax appraisal cards collection. These images, which the county used to document and tax properties throughout their jurisdiction, include numerous buildings along Highway 89 and provide a surprisingly thorough architectural context for the route as it passed through the state's most populous county.

It is an excellent example of the project's reciprocity: the collection gained great content, while a smaller institution was able to take advantage of a platform they could not otherwise develop. "We would have been unable to do this on our own," said the Salt Lake County archivist in an e-mail interview, "so we appreciate any opportunity to partner with larger archives that have staff, much bigger exposure, and the ability to obtain funding for projects such as these" (K. Krattley, personal communication, February 27, 2015).

For Southern Utah University (http://www.li.suu.edu/page/special-collections-about), Highway 89 Digital Collections provided an opportunity to diversify their digital holdings beyond a few dozen CONTENTdm exhibits. According to the department's archivist, their relevant materials include photographs and oral histories related to nearby national parks including Zion, Bryce Canyon, and Grand Canyon. She has just recently been approved to hire a new employee who will help her digitize and upload these materials to the collection.

Like the Salt Lake County Archives, SUU faced some limitations in their ability to upload material to the collection. For one, they did not have the staff in place to create and customize a large-scale Omeka instance, but found the interface "easy to learn and navigate." Due to recent staffing changes, time has been limited and their contribution has not been as large as they would have liked: only twenty-one items at publication. But their archi-

Figure 10.5. Shell Service Station at 962 South State Street in Salt Lake City, UT. *Salt Lake County Archives, Tax Appraisal Cards and Photographs Collection #8-2424*

vist is enthusiastic about expanding her efforts to digitize SUU materials and potentially use the exhibit to reach out to local organizations who might have material related to the road, including the region's Department of Transportation office and the local historical society. "It's been so fun to work with everyone involved and it's been a lot of fun to discover new materials that pertain to Highway 89," she stated, adding, "Yes, research can be fun" (P. Mitchell, personal communication, February 27, 2015).

While the Salt Lake County Archives and Southern Utah University agreed to participate in the Highway 89 exhibit from the beginning, project organizers reached out to the Brigham City Museum (http://collections.boxeldermuseum.org/) after the website was up and running. This was the first step in an effort to incorporate material from even smaller institutions, and for this purpose the museum, located in Brigham City, Utah, was an ideal fit. They had partnered with nearby Utah State University on previous projects, and despite limited hours and part-time staff, had already developed a digital presence for their materials.

While enthusiastic about the project, the museum was concerned that they did not have much material to contribute. As a result, Utah State University offered to collaborate with them on an exhibit related to Peach Days, a local festival, and a segment of Highway 89 known as "The Fruit Way," famous for the produce grown and sold along the roadside. By combining efforts, the two institutions will be able to create more exhaustive exhibits and rely on each other for technical and collection expertise.

Together, these three case studies show the successes and challenges of building a digital exhibit geared toward the involvement of smaller institutions. Some, like the Salt Lake County Archive, jumped right in, identifying, digitizing, and uploading content at a faster rate than their larger peers. Others, like the Brigham City Museum, were encouraged to participate through a collaborative effort with one of the larger institutions. The lesson is this: Each institution's situation is unique, and organizing members need to display flexibility in providing a reasonable level of support and cooperation.

One of the unique things about a collaborative exhibit like the Highway 89 Digital Collection is that advertising is necessary not only to attract passive website traffic, but also active contributors, both institutional and individual. To accomplish this task, representatives from the organizing institutions utilized promotional material, presentations, publications, and social media to draw over 6,000 new users to the site between November 2013 and February 2015. In some cases, these promotional efforts coincided with a significant spike in web traffic as well as additional publicity and contributions.

The idea for promotional materials was conceived by the ILEAD team, which used the program's small grant to commission a piece of Highway 89–themed art. After presenting about the project at a regional archives conference in Salt Lake City, they hired a local graphic designer who, conveniently, had an interest in road history and was already known for his illustrations inspired by the Works Progress Administration's national park posters. This style meshed perfectly with the spirit of the Highway 89 Digital Collection, and the ILEAD team eagerly enlisted the artist's services. The resulting illustration featured a vintage Ford Galaxy cruising the road past Utah's Loafer Mountain, with the phrase "Highway to Grandeur" and, of course, a link to the digital exhibit. One of the organizing institutions then paid for a run of two hundred posters and three thousand postcards, which were placed in special collections reading rooms and visitors centers across the state.

Members of the ILEAD team also made the rounds at local, regional, and national gatherings to promote the Highway 89 Digital Collection. Audiences included annual conference-goers from the Conference of Intermountain Archivists, the Utah State Historical Society, and the Best Practices Exchange. Project organizers also spoke to staff at local museums and historical societies from communities and counties along the route. In addition to these talks, the Highway 89 team submitted a write-up to the *Utah Historical Quarterly*, which provided a detailed description of the project's scope and featured an image from its collections. The article resulted in a spike in the website's traffic, bringing nearly two hundred new visits shortly after its release.

Other advertising involved less traditional methods. Project organizers created a Highway 89 Digital Collections Facebook page (https://www.facebook.com/highway89), which they periodically update with new online exhibits and news stories featuring the road. Participating institutions often shared this content through their social media outlets or made their own posts about the project. These efforts alone funneled nearly five hundred new users to the site, or about 8 percent of the total.

These advertising efforts resulted in some unsolicited media coverage. A stack of the postcards available at Weber State University's Special Collections sparked a conversation between staff and a reporter for the Ogden, Utah, *Standard-Examiner* who was doing research there. The resulting article drove some three hundred fifty new users to the website. This combination of word-of-mouth and print advertising also alerted the city of Orem, Utah, to the online exhibit, to which they enthusiastically contributed two home movies filmed while driving down the highway in the 1940s and 1960s.

Clearly, advertising is an essential part of drawing traffic to a digital exhibit and attracting potential contributors. Posters and postcards featuring an appealing illustration proved to be a fruitful passive strategy, attracting unexpected attention through media coverage and contributions. Written promotion—geared specifically toward local history enthusiasts through the state history journal and generally to the public through newspapers—was a particularly successful active strategy that resulted in noticeable spikes in

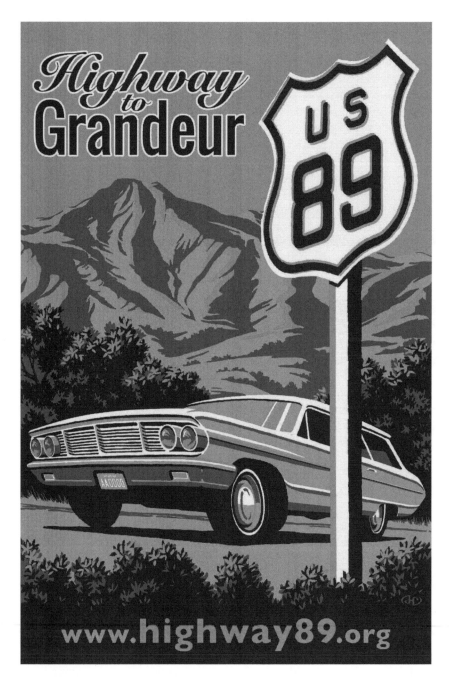

Figure 10.6.   Promotional poster for Highway 89 Digital Collections. *Illustration by John Clark*

web traffic. Although Highway 89 exhibit organizers did not think to do it during the project's first year, this latter finding would suggest that composing a press release for local media would be a beneficial approach in the future.

After two years of collaboration, the Highway 89 partners feel that they have developed a functional and attractive web presence with a simple back-end interface that fosters participation from institutions both large and small. At publication, the project boasted nine contributing institutions that have collectively uploaded 1,375 items. While this is a promising start, there is still a great deal of work to be done. The next phases of the project include expanding the partner base to include more institutions beyond Utah, and encouraging contributions from the general public through crowdsourcing or donations of physical materials.

Highway 89's geographic range encompasses a diverse set of landscapes and cultures that are documented by an equally diverse set of museums and archives. Stretching from Arizona into Utah, Idaho, Wyoming, and Montana, these institutions, large and small, are certain to have unique materials to contribute to the digital collection. By taking advantage of professional networking through working relationships and events like workshops and regional conferences, the organizing members hope to expand participation up and down the route. While support will be available from USU, additional collaborators should have no trouble uploading and describing their own digital materials given the ease with which Utah institutions have done so to this point.

In addition to institutions in other states, the organizing members want to encourage contributions from members of the general public. The idea is to allow members of the general public to submit content directly to the website using a separate process from the institutional contributors. Currently, the Highway 89 Digital Collections page utilizes an Omeka plugin that allows users to upload content by clicking on a tab that reads "contribute an item." The user is then prompted to choose whether they are uploading a story, image, or video; this selection then takes them to a page with the appropriate metadata fields for that object. As with other content, these items are described using Dublin Core, but additional explanations are provided for each field to make sure they are clear to users. For example, instead of simply "rights," the field is labeled with the question: "Who owns the rights to this item and how should they be contacted if there are more questions?"

Obviously, some safety precautions had to be instituted to prevent unwanted activity, but these steps were kept to a minimum so as not to discourage potential contributors. The main tool for this purpose is a registration page, which asks for just four items: username, display name, e-mail, and password. There is also a reCAPTCHA key to prevent spamming. Once these fields are filled in, the user can contribute the item, which must first be

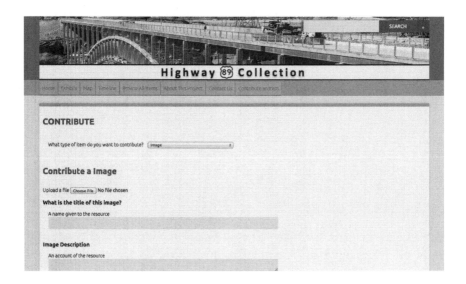

Figure 10.7.   Highway 89 Digital Collections portion of contributor page

approved by a site administrator; however, the contributions plugin automatically e-mails the contributor a thank-you note and a link to their item, which they can see as long as they are logged in. So, even though the public can't see the item, the contributor still gets that "immediate reward" effect. Though the contribution tab has not been up long enough to see much use, the successful use of such methods by similar projects suggests a great potential for success. The Route 66 Flickr page has received some sixteen hundred user-submitted images in the six years it has been up.

While the primary goal of the Highway 89 Digital Collections is to aggregate digital photographs and documents, another hope is that it will also lead to the donation of physical materials. Archivists often use digital exhibits to entice potential donors by demonstrating the institution's ability to make online surrogates available to a global audience. The Highway 89 exhibit gives this advantage to smaller museums and archives that might not otherwise be able to host online content.

With an online presence that is easy for researchers and the general public to navigate and simple interfaces through which institutions and the public can upload content, the Highway 89 Digital Collections offers an excellent template for cultural institutions looking to collaborate with a diverse set of partners. This project demonstrates how a digital exhibit can bridge the gap between large institutions and their smaller counterparts in a way that does not highlight inequalities in resources and technical skills, but bypasses them. Similarly, it breaks down barriers between archives and users by allowing the public to invest in the collection through virtual donations. In these ways, the Highway 89 Digital Collection puts institutions of all sizes and their users on equal footing, in a sense "democratizing digital."

NOTE

1. The Utah Manuscript Association began in the 1980s as a venue for the larger Utah university special collections curators and the LDS Church Archives to meet and discuss collecting efforts. Over the years the membership of this group has grown to include archivists who work at municipal, county, and state archives; religious archives; and smaller academic institutions.

REFERENCES

Barthuli, Kaisa, Jennifer Day, and Sean Evans. 2012. "Route 66 Archives and Research Collaborative," Presented at Society of Southwest Archivists and Conference of Intermountain Archivists Joint Conference, May 23, 2012, Mesa Arizona.

Index

About the Editor and Contributors

Bradford Lee Eden is dean of library services at Valparaiso University. He is editor of *OCLC Systems and Services: Digital Library Perspectives International; The Bottom Line: Managing Library Finances; Library Leadership and Management*, the journal of the Library Leadership & Management Association (LLAMA) within the American Library Association; and the *Journal of Tolkien Research*, a new, open-access peer-reviewed journal. He is also on the editorial boards of *Library Hi Tech*, *Advances in Library Administration and Organization*, and the *Journal of Film Music*. He has a master's and PhD degrees in musicology as well as an MS in library science. His two books *Innovative Redesign and Reorganization of Library Technical Services: Paths for the Future and Case Studies* (2004) and *More Innovative Redesign and Reorganization of Library Technical Services* (2009) are used and cited extensively in the field. His recent books include *Middle-Earth Minstrel: Essays on Music in Tolkien* (2010), *The Associate University Librarian Handbook: A Resource Guide* (Scarecrow Press, 2012), *Leadership in Academic Libraries: Connecting Theory to Practice* (Scarecrow Press, 2014), and *The Hobbit and Tolkien's Mythology: Essays on Revisions and Influences* (2014).

* * *

Kathryn Barwick works in collection development at the State Library of New South Wales. From 2012 to 2014 she worked on the library's social media-focused Innovation Project exploring how social media could be used to share library collections, engage with the community, and encourage creativity and interactivity.

Tracy C. Bergstrom is the codirector of the Digital Initiatives and Scholarship Program within the Hesburgh Libraries of Notre Dame. As such, she oversees digital production, outreach on behalf of digital services, and grants development. She is also the curator of the Zahm Dante and early Italian imprints collection at Notre Dame and is especially interested in the print history of Dante's *Divine Comedy.*

Kaela Casey began her career in libraries as a student assistant at the Ventura College Library. After completing her BA in art, she worked in several staff positions at the John Spoor Broome Library at California State University, Channel Islands. Kaela is a 2009 ALA Spectrum Scholar and received her MLIS from San Jose State University in 2012. She is currently the public and electronic services librarian at the John Spoor Broome Library at California State University Channel Islands.

Joe C. Clark is the head of the Performing Arts Library at Kent State University. His research interests include information-seeking behavior, user experience, and the changing nature of scholarly information. He is active in the American Library Association, Association of College and Research Libraries, the Music Library Association.

Brad Cole is currently the interim dean at the Utah State University Libraries. He received a master's degree in history from Utah State University in 1986 and holds certification in the Academy of Certified Archivists. Cole worked as the manuscript curator at Northern Arizona University from 1995 to 2005. He has been associate dean for special collections at Merrill-Cazier Library since 2005.

Karen Evans is a reference, instruction, and government publications librarian at Indiana State University. She holds and MLS and a graduate degree in criminology and criminal justice. She serves as the librarian for criminology and criminal justice.

Teri Gallaway is the library systems and Web coordinator at the Monroe Library, Loyola University New Orleans.

Joyce Garczynski is Towson University's communications and development librarian. In this role she teaches communication students about the research process, manages publicity and social media for the library, and writes library fundraising appeals, as well. Joyce received her MLS from the University of Maryland's iSchool in 2009 and holds a master's degree in communication research from the University of Pennsylvania.

Mylee Joseph is a consultant to the network of public libraries across New South Wales. From 2012 to 2014 she was the project leader for the Innovation Project at the State Library of New South Wales, exploring the potential of digital engagement for delivering library services, building digital engagement skills in library teams using social media tools, and integrating mobile technology into delivering library services via the 23 Mobile Things project.

Elizabeth Kelly is the digital initiatives librarian at the Monroe Library, Loyola University New Orleans.

Dana McKay is not a librarian (though she is often mistaken for one). Her background is in computer science, human computer interaction, and digital libraries, in which she has a master's degree. For the past eight years she has worked as a user experience practitioner at Swinburne University of Technology, predominantly in the library (though she can occasionally be found trying to improve the Swinburne website too). Her work in the library has included problems as diverse as institutional repository usability, how readers interact with e-books, how to approach the offerings of web-scale search and discovery, what readers do at the shelves, and how library users use library space. Dana has a long-standing interest in how people actually look for and use information (as opposed to what the system says they should do), and is working on a PhD at the University of Melbourne in how to improve online browsing opportunities. In her spare time she reverse-engineers airport processes, public transport ticketing systems, consumer packaging, and the irritating self-checkout machines at the supermarket, wondering why their designers never thought about the people who would eventually use them.

Alexander Papson is the head of the Digital Projects Unit in the Digital Initiatives and Scholarship Program within the Hesburgh Libraries of Notre Dame. As such, he oversees digital production and rights management for digital projects. He is also the metadata and digital projects librarian.

Rebecca Parker is the manager, Information Management Projects at Swinburne University of Technology, where she is responsible for delivering the university's enterprise content management strategy. She is leading a university-wide program to improve enterprise information management, developing support and capability, and implementing new systems to support improved practice. Rebecca was previously Swinburne's inaugural research services librarian, where she played a leading role in the establishment of the library's services to researchers. She has extensive expertise in corporate information management, institutional repositories, copyright and intellectual property, metadata, metrics, data management, online publishing support, and research profile management and promotion. Like many librarians, she is an avid reader, a knitter, and an amateur ukulele player.

Clint Pumphrey is the manuscript curator in the Special Collections and Archives division of Utah State University's Merrill-Cazier Library. A 2009 graduate of USU's master's program in history, he now manages over five hundred archival collections and serves on the Utah State Historical Records Advisory Board and the *Utah Historical Quarterly* advisory board of editors. Among his research interests are environmental and leisure history, which has led to a publication and numerous presentations about tourism and ecology along U.S. Highway 89.

Laksamee Putnam is the science librarian at the Albert S. Cook Library at Towson University where she serves as library liaison to the Biology, Molecular Biology, Chemistry, Forensic Chemistry, and Environmental Science Departments. She obtained her undergraduate degree in environmental biology from the University of Colorado, and a master's in library and information science from the University of Illinois Urbana-Champaign. She is an active member of ACRL—Science and Technology Section and the Maryland Library Association. Her research focus is on use of emerging technologies and social media to increase science education on all levels, to the public, between scientists, and beyond. Her online portfolio is available here: https://sites.google.com/site/putnamlis/.

Brian Sullivan is the instructional and research technologies librarian at the Monroe Library, Loyola University New Orleans.

Susan Van Alstyne is the Newark Campus library director at Berkeley College. She earned a BS in business administration from New Jersey City University, and holds an MLIS from Florida State University. Ms. Van Alstyne has worked in the field of information management for over twenty years with library experience in corporate, public, and academic settings.

Malia Willey is the instruction coordinator at the Monroe Library, Loyola University New Orleans.

Liz Woolcott serves as the head of Cataloging and Metadata Services at Utah State University. Prior to this position, she worked as the digital discovery librarian, specializing in the implementation of metadata standards and workflows for digital cultural heritage objects. She serves as cochair of the Mountain West Digital Library Geospatial Discovery Task Force, which develops collaborative standards for recording geographical metadata, and as the president of the Cache Valley Library Association. She has an MLS from the University of North Texas and an MA in History from Utah State University.

Laura Worden kicked off her college library career while working on her BA in history at California State University, Northridge. During this time, she was given the opportunity to help build a library for the new twenty-third campus of the Cal State system. After receiving her MLIS from San Jose State University, she took a position as a librarian at the John Spoor Broome Library at California State University, Channel Islands. In addition to an MLIS, Laura has a post-master's certificate in library and information science from San Jose State University. Currently she is the original cataloging and public services librarian at the Broome Library.

Lisa Woznicki is the performing arts librarian at the Albert S. Cook Library at Towson University, where she serves as library liaison to the Dance, Music, and Theatre Arts Departments. She also teaches Women in Western Music as an adjunct instructor in the Department of Music. She has undergraduate degrees in English literature and music from Towson University, as well as master's degrees in library science and music education from the University of Maryland, College Park, and Towson University, respectively. She is a member of the Music Library Association, the Theatre Library Association, the Congress on Research and Dance, and the International Association of Women in Music. She has recently published articles in the *Journal of Performing Arts Leadership in Higher Education* and the *Journal of the IAWM: International Alliance for Women in Music*.